MW01205999

LUMINALIBRIA

DOLORES CANNON: THE GREAT COMPENDIUM OF HER WORK.
FROM HIDDEN DIMENSIONS TO LIFE BEYOND DEATH

50 YEARS IN THE PURSUIT OF UNDERSTANDING THE MEANING AND ORIGIN OF EXISTENCE

LUMINALIBRIA

DEDICATION

To all those who seek with an open heart and a curious mind: this book is dedicated to you. May Dolores Cannon's journey inspire every step of your path towards a profound understanding of life, the universe, and our existence. May her wisdom guide you through the mysteries of time and space, leading you to discoveries illuminated by love and knowledge. In honor of Dolores, a pioneer of the unknown, a guide on the soul's journey.

LUMINALIBRIA

With all our respect and admiration

CONTENTS

INTRODUCTION

Welcome to the extraordinary and captivating world of Dolores Cannon, a figure who has left an indelible mark on the landscape of human consciousness exploration. This book, "Dolores Cannon: The Great Compendium of Her Work - From Hidden Dimensions to Life Beyond Death - 50 years in the pursuit of understanding the meaning and origin of existence," represents a journey through half a century of groundbreaking research, discoveries, and insights.

Dolores Cannon, through her unique technique of regression hypnosis (QHHT), opened doors to worlds that many considered inaccessible. With a meticulous and passionate approach, she delved into the depths of the human mind, uncovering stories of past lives, extraterrestrial contacts, vanished civilizations like Atlantis, and tackled the mystery of life beyond death with a perspective that challenges our deepest beliefs.

Within these pages, you will find a comprehensive compendium of Dolores's work, a body of work that condenses five decades of research and clinical practice. From her initial explorations with her husband Johnny Cannon to insights into phenomena like the three waves of volunteers and the vision of a New Earth, this book is a tribute to her unrelenting quest for truth and understanding.

Through her numerous case studies, Dolores touched the lives of thousands of people, offering new perspectives on universal questions: Who are we? Where do we come from? What awaits us after death? Her theories, sometimes controversial, have always sparked debate and encouraged many to ponder the deeper meaning of our existence.

Dolores Cannon's work stands out not only for its academic and clinical value but also for its ability to touch the hearts and souls of those seeking answers. This book is more than just a collection of theories and stories; it is an invitation to explore the unknown and see the world and oneself in an entirely new light.

Within these pages, we invite you to embark on a journey beyond time and space, a path of inner discovery and expanded consciousness. May this book be a source of inspiration, reflection, and wonder for you, just as it has been for all those who have had the privilege of embarking on the unique journey offered by Dolores Cannon.

BIOGRAPHY

Dolores Cannon, born in 1931, was an internationally renowned hypnotherapist and author whose life and work deeply influenced the field of human consciousness exploration. Her career was marked by tireless research into the mysteries of existence, a passion shared and fueled by her collaboration with her husband, Johnny Cannon.

The couple began their journey into hypnosis in the 1960s, a time when this practice was still met with skepticism and surrounded by an aura of mystery. Initially, their interest was focused on hypnosis as a therapeutic tool to help people quit smoking or lose weight. However, their insatiable curiosity led them far beyond traditional applications, pushing them to explore the unknown boundaries of the human mind.

The pivotal moment in their career came with the discovery of regression hypnosis, which allowed people to access memories of past lives. This revolutionary approach opened a new chapter in the understanding of human nature, challenging conventions and laying the foundation for unprecedented exploration of the mysteries of life and consciousness.

After Johnny's premature death, Dolores continued the work they had started together with unwavering determination, becoming a prominent figure in the field of regression hypnosis. With her innovative approach and revelations, she garnered the attention of a wide international audience, sparking curiosity and inspiring many to embark on their own journey of inner discovery.

In addition to her professional role, Dolores had a rich and fulfilling family life. She and Johnny were loving parents, and their family played a crucial role in their lives. Family support was essential for Dolores, especially after her husband's passing, providing her with the strength and motivation to continue her work and research.

Johnny Cannon was not only Dolores's husband and life partner but also an essential figure in the development of her early techniques. Their collaboration laid the groundwork for the work that defined Dolores's career and her legacy in the field of regression hypnosis.

After Johnny's passing, Dolores carried on their mission with the Quantum Healing Hypnosis Technique (QHHT), a method that uses a deep state of hypnosis to allow clients to explore memories of past lives and receive insights from a higher consciousness. This technique became a cornerstone in her practice and offered new perspectives on the nature of reality and human existence.

Dolores Cannon lived an extraordinary life, successfully balancing her roles as a professional, wife, and mother. Her dedication to both family and work served as an inspiration to many, demonstrating that it is possible to pursue a professional passion while maintaining a strong and loving bond with loved ones.

Her contribution to the world of regression hypnosis and the exploration of human consciousness remains unparalleled. Dolores left a lasting legacy through her numerous books, covering a wide range of topics, from past lives to reincarnation, from UFOs to ancient civilizations. Her works generated widespread interest, dividing public opinion between admiration and criticism but always stimulating reflection and exploration.

Dolores Cannon, with her pioneering work, left an indelible mark in the field of human consciousness exploration, making her a prominent figure within her field and beyond. Her legacy continues to inspire and guide those seeking to understand the mysteries of the soul and human existence. Dolores left her physical body in 2014, after dedicating her life to helping her patients and researching the meaning of our existences, the true history, and origin of humanity.

THE SOUL'S JOURNEY: LESSONS ON LIFE, KARMA, AND TRANSCENDENCE

Dolores Cannon, in her approach to researching life after death, openly and in detail discusses her findings, which align with the teachings of various religions, such as Hinduism. In her book "Between Death and Life," she explores topics she has also delved into in ashrams around the world, revealing a universal connection among various faiths regarding her theories.

Throughout her career, Dolores Cannon conducted thousands of past-life regression sessions. This process, as she explained, also involves guiding clients through the experience of death. Contrary to the claims of some hypnosis schools that consider this passage dangerous, she asserts that if done correctly, this procedure is safe and even enlightening. Through this method, she was able to uncover the origins of phobias, allergies, and medical issues in clients' current lives, often stemming from how they died in their past lives.

According to Dolores Cannon, descriptions of the death experience provided by her clients are remarkably similar, regardless of their personal stories. These descriptions do not match the numerous and well-known near-death experiences but rather what she calls the "real death." People report an initial sensation of cold, followed by the perception of being outside their body, looking down at the bed. This passage is described as rapid and straightforward, a gentle transition from one position to another.

After leaving the body, people express a sense of liberation and a desire to move forward, leaving behind the limitations of the physical body. Dolores Cannon emphasizes that souls do not wish to return to their bodies, especially if they are sick or suffering. Furthermore, she reinforces the concept that those in mourning should let go of their deceased loved ones, as returning to a sick or suffering body would be selfish.

In her enlightening book, Dolores Cannon also addresses the concept of a pre-birth "contract" or life plan. According to her, each person has agreed to a pre-established plan before birth, which includes a predetermined moment to leave this life. All of this suggests that death is never a random event but an integral part of a much larger plan.

The book also discusses the presence of guides or guardian angels who accompany each individual, both in life and in death. These spiritual entities, which can be guardian angels or deceased loved ones, are assigned to assist the individual throughout their life. Dolores Cannon reassures that no one is ever alone, neither in life nor in death, and these guides are always present to provide support and guidance. She then outlines her perceptions of near-death experiences (NDEs) and the difference between these and real death. When speaking publicly, she often liked to inquire about participants' near-death experiences, emphasizing that such experiences are very real, despite the opinions of some medical and professional skeptics.

According to Dolores Cannon, near-death experiences (NDEs) often involve the sensation of passing through a tunnel or leaving the body, approaching a bright light. However, in these experiences, people usually never reach the light and are often brought back before reaching it. This contrasts with real death, where one does pass through the light. Dolores describes this light as a powerful source of energy, akin to God, and underscores that during real death, the silver cord connecting the spirit to the body is severed, marking a point of no return.

She also presents the idea that the spirit, a person's true self, leaves the body every night during sleep. These nightly journeys include visits to the spiritual side, where one communicates with guides and masters and embarks on adventures in various parts of the world or even other planets and dimensions. However, these journeys often remain unknown, with only fragments of memories emerging in the form of flying dreams or unfamiliar places.

One of the most important concepts expressed by Dolores Cannon is that life on Earth is like a school, where the primary lessons are emotions and limitations, concepts not taught on other planets. She emphasizes that Earth is a highly challenging learning environment, and the souls here are in a continuous learning process. Another important concept derived from her teachings is that the notion of hell is a pure invention of the church and has no basis in the afterlife she investigated. It is evident that a loving God would not punish the souls He created, but rather allow them to make mistakes and learn from them, reincarnating repeatedly until they have fully learned all necessary lessons. That's why she often emphasizes that life, in this view, appears as a series of lessons, and the real difficulty is that, once reincarnated, we forget the reason we came to Earth.

According to transcripts from the sessions of regression hypnosis by Cannon, three different "places" in the afterlife are described, places that souls can visit based on their vibration and frequency. The first is the "lower astral," where souls anchored to Earth reside. These souls, often people who lived negative lives as criminals or were addicted to alcohol, smoking, drugs, remain confused and do not realize they have died. They continue to seek the same earthly sensations and are in a state of denial. However, over time, these souls realize that they need to move forward and are always greeted with love once they decide to do so.

The "middle astral" is the second place described. It can be equated to what many religions call heaven. This place is described as extremely beautiful, with lakes, hills, houses of various shapes and sizes, and gardens with vibrant colors. Here, souls can create their version of paradise, living in dream homes or castles, surrounded by deceased friends and family. Dolores emphasizes that the colors and beauty of this place are beyond earthly imagination, with flowers that never wither and nature that surpasses Earth's in beauty.

These descriptions highlight the view of an afterlife with different layers, where earthly experiences and choices influence where a soul may reside after death. These ideas emphasize the importance of choices made during life and their significant impact on the afterlife experience. In the "middle astral," souls live what appears to be a perfect life, immersed in idyllic settings where they can reunite with their deceased loved ones and fulfill their deepest desires. However, it is specified that this phase is temporary and does not represent the end of the soul's journey.

The experience in the middle astral is destined to change when the time for the so-called "life review" arrives. This process requires souls to examine every aspect of their earthly life in detail. During this review, souls not only relive their actions but also the reactions and emotions of those around them. This experience can be intensely painful, as it brings to light even the unintended consequences of one's actions and words. Dolores Cannon's works emphasize the importance of this awareness, suggesting that it can certainly lead people to live with greater kindness and understanding in their earthly lives.

In the context of life after death according to Dolores Cannon's view, the theme of karma and reincarnation is also explored. Souls, realizing their past actions, may choose to reincarnate to "correct" mistakes and learn from past experiences. This process is described as a role-playing "game," where souls negotiate with each other to define the roles they will assume in the next life to balance past experiences and promote spiritual growth.

This process is illustrated with concrete examples, such as souls deciding to reverse the roles of parent and child or partner in different lives, in order to better experience and understand different perspectives. This approach reflects the author's view of earthly life as a stage, where souls wear temporary "costumes " to play specific roles. Life, therefore, is seen as a series of acts, with souls taking on different roles in different lives.

Finally, we talk about the "upper astral," describing it as a place of learning and knowledge. Here, souls have access to schools and institutions like the Temple of Wisdom, where they can deepen their understanding of the universe and their own existence. Dolores Cannon's attraction to this level reflects her desire for knowledge and understanding, highlighting her curiosity and continuous commitment to research.

In short, Dolores Cannon's ideas outline a soul's journey that goes far beyond earthly life, proposing a process of continuous evolution and learning through various phases and levels of existence. She goes on to describe her vision of the afterlife, illustrating the existence of a so-called "tapestry of life." This tapestry, as she describes it, is a visual metaphor representing the complexity and interweaving of human lives. Each person has their own thread in the tapestry, representing the course of their life. She emphasizes how these threads intertwine with each other, demonstrating how each individual influences and is influenced by others. This tapestry symbolizes the interconnectedness of all lives, emphasizing the importance of everyone's actions and words in influencing the overall pattern.

Another important concept that emerges from Dolores Cannon's regression hypnosis sessions is the absence of prejudice and judgment in the afterlife. With an understanding of interconnection and mutual influence, the fundamental equality of all souls is recognized. Each soul is at a different stage of its development and is attending different "classes" in the school of life.

There is also a great library in the afterlife, which the scholar describes as her favorite place. In this library, which contains every imaginable piece of information, Dolores says she obtained much of the information used in her books. This library not only preserves knowledge of everything that has happened but also of what will happen. The Akashic records are also mentioned, accessible in this place, and the library is described as an environment where knowledge can be explored in various ways, including direct experience in rooms that simulate specific scenarios, similar to Star Trek's "Holodeck."

The theme of schools in the upper astral is also explained in great detail. In these "schools," souls can learn any imaginable subject, in line with their curiosity and interests. However, it is emphasized that learning in the upper astral, while vast, cannot replace the practical experience of earthly life. Learning through direct experience, with all its emotional challenges, is seen as a more effective and rapid path to soul growth. Through these vivid descriptions, the afterlife appears as a place of infinite knowledge and learning, where every soul has the opportunity to grow and evolve through various experiences, both in astral and earthly forms. Schools, the library, and the tapestry of life represent different aspects of this ongoing evolution, where souls learn not only through the acquisition of knowledge but also through direct experience and interaction with other souls.

Dolores Cannon further emphasizes the importance of practical experience in life, comparing it to theoretical learning. She argues in her book that, just as in a chemistry lab or the mechanics of a car, theory alone is not sufficient to fully understand a subject. This metaphor extends to earthly life: we can read and learn concepts like love, hate, or jealousy, but it is only through experiencing them directly that we can fully comprehend them. That's why souls choose to reincarnate on Earth: to learn more quickly, repay their karma, and complete their spiritual journey more efficiently.

In the exposition of her description of the soul's journey after physical death, the process of reincarnation planning is important, and it is described in all detail how souls make "contracts" with other souls before birth. Contrary to what many believe, there is no divine judge determining people's destinies; rather, each soul writes its own "life script." This process includes choosing family and social roles, as well as life scenarios. Dolores strongly emphasizes the idea that each soul is its own harshest judge, reviewing its own life and deciding what to repay through karma.

On a practical level, every soul arrives on Earth with a well-defined plan, which she describes as "wrapped like a Christmas gift." However, free will and the plans of others lead to collisions and deviations from these ideal scenarios. This complexity is an integral part of earthly life and contributes to its unpredictability and challenges. The concept of forgetfulness is also important: when souls incarnate on Earth, they forget their pre-existing plans and connections, making life a true "test." Children, in the early years of life, are described as beings who are forgetting their previous life, while elderly people, before dying, receive their "final instructions."

The theme of death is also part of every soul's life plan. Each person decides how and when they will die, even though this decision is not conscious during earthly life. Death is seen as a planned passage, an exit from a physical body that is no longer needed, and not as a random or unfortunate event. According to Dolores Cannon's extensive hypnosis sessions, every person plans not only their own life but also the way and timing of their own death. This planning is likened to a conscious choice, just as deciding to participate in an event where many people die. She emphasizes that events like earthquakes or disasters, such as those on September 11th, are not random but part of soul-level agreements.

Also important is the issue of control over one's life. Dolores argues that once people understand that they have created the circumstances of their lives, they can also change them. This understanding confers power and responsibility because it implies that people are not victims of circumstances but rather co-creators of their own reality.

Furthermore, through her research, we can also understand how souls decide on their life path before reincarnating. This process includes the choice of gender, place of birth, and other life conditions. Sometimes, souls try to take on too much in one life, which can lead to a particularly challenging life. Spiritual guides can offer advice, but the final choice lies with the soul itself.

In this process, the veil of forgetfulness that covers souls when they reincarnate also appears. This veil prevents people from remembering their pre-birth plans and their past lives, making earthly life a true test of growth and development. Souls, at the moment of death, have a revelation, remembering their plans and understanding the meaning of their lives.

Also interesting is learning from Dolores Cannon about sleep paralysis experiences and out-of-body experiences. She explains that these phenomena are related to the connection between the physical body and the soul. These experiences are normal and should not be a source of fear.

After death, souls can also have a special role, that of assisting their loved ones remaining on Earth or reincarnating to help others. This concept is in line with the underlying idea that death is not the end but rather a passage to another existence. This idea strongly emerges from the research of this extraordinary researcher in the field of spirituality.

Also interesting is her reflection on premature deaths, such as those of children or infants. She explains that these souls have chosen a short life for a specific reason, often to teach something to those left behind. This perspective offers comfort to those who have lost loved ones, suggesting that every life, no matter how short, has a purpose and deeper meaning. Dolores Cannon, speaking of how everyone has a personal plan for their life, emphasizes the importance of reactions and influences from these experiences on personal growth. Every person, she says, has a role to play in their own life plan, and the key lies in understanding how one is influenced by these experiences and what is learned from them.

Delving into this fascinating subject, the esteemed researcher addresses the issue of people born with severe illnesses or disabilities. She explains that these conditions are not random accidents but conscious choices made by the soul before birth. According to her, souls choose to be born with these conditions because they offer unique opportunities to "repair" more karma in one life than would be possible in many others. These lives not only provide deep learning experiences for the soul living with the condition but also for those who interact with them, such as family members and caregivers. The presence of these individuals in the lives of others is a powerful teaching on how to react to difficulty and suffering.

The theme of near-death experiences is also explained in great detail, especially negative ones. These experiences are often the result of a person's expectations and beliefs. If a person is conditioned to believe in the existence of hell or to feel unworthy, they may have a negative near-death experience. However, Dolores reassures that these experiences are not definitive and are strongly influenced only by personal expectations.

Explaining the impact of religious beliefs on death, Cannon highlights how church conditioning can influence the perception of death and the afterlife. She recounts, in her writings, the stories of elderly people who die in fear because of the belief that they have not been perfect and therefore deserve punishment. She argues that it is important to free oneself from these fears because the reality of the afterlife is very different from these misguided earthly conceptions.

Also interesting is the story of a friend of hers who assisted her dying mother. This story illustrates how souls can choose to stay on Earth longer than expected to take care of someone or to complete a certain experience. Her friend's mother, for example, delayed her own death out of concern for her daughter, demonstrating how the soul's plan can sometimes adapt to earthly circumstances. At a critical moment, when it seemed that her mother had passed away, her friend prayed intensely, and unexpectedly her mother resumed breathing. This event allowed her mother to live for another year, during which her friend significantly improved her life by buying a house and preparing for the future. Her friend's mother then passed away exactly one year later, on the same day her father had died 15 years earlier, suggesting a sort of predestined or chosen timing.

Through these examples and reflections, we can realize the complexity and depth of soul choices, showing how every life experience, whether joyful or painful, has a deeper spiritual meaning in the soul's path towards growth and evolution. Each individual has their own life path that has been carefully planned before birth, and this path is not only a collection of personal experiences but also an opportunity to influence and teach others. Every reaction and interaction thus becomes a significant part of one's journey of growth and learning.

These reflections and stories that Dolores has left us illustrate a complex and multifaceted panorama of human existence, where every choice, challenge, and relationship has a profound spiritual significance. The soul's vision presented by Cannon is that of an entity in continuous evolution, which through a variety of experiences, both positive and painful, learns vital lessons and contributes to the collective growth of all souls.

To conclude this section of the book that has dealt with a very important aspect of Dolores Cannon's work, I want to summarize her findings about karma and its influence on people's lives and their relationships:

Reincarnation and Karma: Dolores Cannon argues that souls reincarnate multiple times. In each life, an individual may encounter the same souls with whom they have had significant interactions in past lives. These relationships can be influenced by accumulated karma, which is the result of actions and decisions made in previous incarnations.

Life Lessons: According to Cannon, each life is a series of learned lessons. Karma acts as a balancing mechanism, ensuring that each soul faces situations that allow them to learn and grow. This may explain why some people face similar challenges or encounter similar types of people repeatedly in their lives.

Karma Resolution: A crucial aspect of Cannon's ideas is that karma is not punishment but rather an opportunity for learning and growth. Souls can resolve karma through positive actions, understanding, and forgiveness of others and themselves. Resolving karma is fundamental to the spiritual evolution of the soul.

Soul Contracts: Cannon also speaks of "soul contracts," agreements made between souls before birth. These contracts outline key experiences and lessons that an individual will have to face in life. These contracts are often linked to karma, as souls may choose to experience certain situations to resolve past karma.

Cross-Influences: Karmic connections not only affect individual lives but also relationship dynamics. For example, a difficult relationship in one life may be the result of unresolved conflict in a previous life, leading souls to reincarnate together to address and resolve these issues.

Healing and Growth: Cannon emphasizes that understanding and working through one's karmic connections can lead to profound healing and personal growth. By opening the mind to these connections, people can begin to see life's challenges as opportunities to break free from karmic cycles and progress spiritually.

In summary, Dolores Cannon's ideas about karmic connections offer a perspective that sees life as a journey of learning, where every experience and relationship has a deeper meaning linked to the soul's growth and evolution. Through this process, souls have the opportunity to resolve old conflicts, learn vital lessons, and progress toward a greater spiritual understanding.

THE MIND AND THE POWER OF CREATION: PSYCHIC EXPLORATIONS AND ALTERNATIVE REALITIES

During a significant moment in her career, renowned researcher and therapist Dolores Cannon ventured into a profound analysis of concepts and theories that push beyond the boundaries of human understanding. In her desire to share her knowledge with as many people as possible, she shared this wealth of discoveries with her audience, recognizing that some of the ideas presented might be difficult to grasp and could raise legitimate questions.

Dolores Cannon's professional origins can be traced back to the 1960s, a time when metaphysics and past life therapies were virtually unknown in the Western world. In this unexplored cultural landscape, she emerged as a pioneer, developing a unique technique of hypnotherapy called "Quantum Healing Hypnosis Technique," which she later taught worldwide.

Initially focused on past life regressions to explore human history, she soon encountered concepts that challenged her beliefs and previous knowledge. Her research primarily relied on hypnosis sessions with clients, during which recurring and significant themes shared by many different people emerged. It was these sessions that allowed her to gather information and assemble a vast mosaic of truly revolutionary knowledge.

One of the first and most significant concepts she confronted was that of simultaneous time. This idea emerged during her work on Nostradamus's prophecies, where she found herself communicating with him across time while the famous seer was still alive. The notion that everything exists simultaneously rather than happening simultaneously is at the core of this theory. Dolores also emphasized the importance of words and terminology in interpreting and understanding these complex concepts.

Her research extended beyond mere historical analysis or the understanding of time. By interacting with what she referred to as the "subconscious mind" or the "higher consciousness" of her patients, she was able to ask questions and receive answers on topics that challenge human understanding. These exchanges allowed her to delve into subjects such as the illusory nature of time and the deeper meaning of our existence. Fascinating, isn't it?

In these hypnosis sessions, it became clear that human understanding of time is an illusion, a concept that binds us to Earth and severely limits our perception of reality. She wryly observed how humanity is probably the only species in the universe that measures something non-existent and stressed the importance of freeing ourselves from these illusory constructs to explore new dimensions of existence.

Dr. Cannon's intellectual and spiritual journey was not

just an exploration of history or the metaphysical but an attempt to decode the complexity of human and universal existence. Through her lectures and publications, she sought to share these revelations with a wider audience, inviting them to join her on this journey of discovery and understanding.

Throughout her career, Dolores Cannon deeply explored the concept of time and reality, discovering that our linear perception of time is actually an illusion, a point she reiterated on many occasions. During one of her public lectures, she discussed how life stages, from childhood to adulthood, coexist simultaneously in a timeless dimension. By using hypnosis, she had observed that it's possible to revisit moments from childhood, demonstrating that these life stages do not disappear but exist concurrently with the present. This is a truly fascinating concept, even though it may not be easy to grasp rationally. She loved to delve into this idea of simultaneous time using the analogy of a phone call between America and London to explain that, despite a six-hour time difference, the conversation still occurs in real-time. This example effectively illustrates how time, as we perceive it, can be deceptive and how, in reality, everything happens simultaneously.

For her, the experience of traveling through different time zones made us experientially realize the non-existence of time. In this way, we can come to understand that our comprehension of time is limited and chaotic, a concept artificially created to structure our daily lives.

In Dolores Cannon's research, there has, of course, been an evolution over the years, a deepening of understanding. She herself admitted that if she had encountered these concepts 30 years earlier, she would have found them too challenging to comprehend and likely would have overlooked them. However, over time, she learned to process this information in small doses, much like feeding a child appropriate food for their age and development.

After writing several books in the "Convoluted Universe" series, she admitted that she thought she had already explored all possible knowledge. Nevertheless, she continued to receive new information that pushed her beyond the boundaries of traditional understanding, forcing her to reconsider and adapt to new concepts.

One of the main and most fascinating topics explored by the hypnotherapist, as previously mentioned, was that of parallel universes and parallel dimensions. She explained in clear and comprehensive terms how every decision made in life creates energy that, when one chooses a path, allows the other alternative choice to create a parallel reality. In these realities, other versions of ourselves live the lives we could have had if we had made different choices. However, according to her conclusions, we should never be aware of these parallel realities, and we should not attempt to explore them to avoid complications and dangerous interference.

In her unparalleled journey to understand the complexity of existence, Dolores always invited her audience to consider these theories with an open mind, pushing the boundaries of their understanding and accepting that there might be more to our linear reality than meets the eye. Through her research, she offered a glimpse into a world of infinite possibilities, encouraging everyone to explore these ideas and reflect on how they might influence our perception of reality.

She hoped that, despite the vast range of existential possibilities, we should focus on the reality we have chosen and currently live, letting the other versions of ourselves continue their independent paths.

Delving into the concept of parallel universes, she showed us that there are thousands of dimensions, each with slight variations from our own, and that we constantly move between these dimensions without realizing it, unless unusual events catch our attention.

Events like the ones she particularly enjoyed recounting. One such event involved a college student who one day saw construction work outside her dormitory, only to discover the next day that there was no trace of such work. Other examples included visions of planes crashing into parallel dimensions and objects seeming to disappear and reappear, suggesting movements between different dimensions.

In one of her most evocative stories, a woman experienced a temporary return to the 1950s, walking down a street where everything seemed to belong to that era, only to return to normalcy once she re-entered her apartment. Other people shared experiences of staying in hotels and visiting gas stations that, the next day, seemed never to have existed. Fascinating, isn't it?

There's also the curious case where a person observed planes and cars moving backward and forward in an unnatural manner, suggesting the presence of a junction point between dimensions where objects were not entirely solid in a single dimension. These stories and reflections presented by Dolores Cannon offer a fascinating and thought-provoking view of the infinite possibilities of our existence, inviting us to consider reality in ways that go beyond our ordinary perception, with different concepts and settings. With her unique approach, she opened a window into a world where the laws of physics and time are much more flexible and mysterious than we could imagine, and profoundly different from commonly known ones.

For her, reality is essentially an illusion created by our minds, with each individual shaping their own world through the power of thought and creation. It's fascinating how she believed that every environment, including the one we find ourselves in right now, did not exist before our decision to be in it.

From this perspective, our life is like a movie or a theater production, where we are the producers, directors, and lead actors. Each person writes their own screenplay as they go through life, with the freedom to change it at will. Understanding the power of the human mind, capable of creating anything from joy to suffering, was of paramount importance to Dolores, and she encouraged everyone to use this power to transform their lives.

Another intriguing aspect of her work is the concept of "background people," an idea also found in the research of Guy Needler. According to this theory, many of the people we encounter in everyday life are actually "extras" in the movie of our life. These background people are not real beings in the traditional sense but are energetic manifestations created by our minds to fill the world around us. On this concept, her sense of humor led her to joke about the idea of creating too many background people in crowded places like airports.

Digging deeper into the theme, Cannon explained that these extras are essential to our life experience because a story without other characters would be dull and monotonous. However, she clarified that these background people do not have their own independent consciousness; they are created for our personal film, adding depth and context to our experience. She loved to compare these holographic entities to characters appearing on the holodeck of Star Trek: they appear real when interacting with them but dissolve as soon as the interaction ends. This concept reflects the idea that many of the interactions and encounters in our lives are guided by a reality constructed and designed for our personal development.

For Dolores, it is essential to understand that it is through the power of our minds that we can consciously start to change our lives and manifest a reality more in line with our desires and aspirations. This discourse has left her readers with new perspectives on life and reality, sparking questions and reflections on the nature of the world around us and our consciousness.

Often in her books, she addressed the theme of the extreme density of our planet, believing it to be one of the most challenging to live on. It is this density that makes life on Earth so demanding and unique in the universe.

It is important to reflect on the illusory nature of reality and the role we play in creating it because this directly reconnects us with the power we have to manifest the reality we want and to evolve over lifetimes.

Returning for a moment to the concept of "background people," Dolores illustrated well how in the "movie" of our existence, we can sometimes assign a more significant role to people who initially seemed to be mere background figures. These characters, who interact with us more deeply, may actually help us on our evolutionary path, just as we can influence them.

These background people, while not having the same

evolutionary complexity as real individuals, can still evolve through interactions with us. In a sort of symbiotic exchange, both we and these energetic entities help each other in our growth and development. This concept overturns our conventional understanding of reality and interpersonal relationships, offering a broader and multidimensional perspective.

Reflecting on the nature of human existence and the role of karma, she delved into how every experience, positive or negative, is a lesson we have chosen to learn. The difficulties and challenges we encounter are intentionally inserted into our life path to help us grow and evolve. She talked about "cyclic karma," a process in which lessons not learned in one life reappear in increasingly challenging forms in subsequent lives until they are understood and assimilated.

That's why it's important to resolve problems and difficult relationships in our current life to avoid repeating the same mistakes in the future. She taught that every individual is responsible for their own evolutionary path and that we must actively confront our problems to move forward.

Although in the past, we faced life's challenges as if we were in elementary school, we are now ready to tackle more complex issues, almost as if we were entering a university of life. This metaphor suggests that humanity is reaching a higher level of understanding and awareness, preparing for more complex and rewarding challenges on our spiritual growth journey.

Addressing the topic of the involvement of the higher self and the oversoul in orchestrating our lives, Cannon clarified that while we operate independently, we are actually part of a larger whole, which is the source. While we create our own reality, we are guided and influenced by our higher selves, which are part of the same universal source.

However, while our perception of reality can be complex and multifaceted, it's important to recognize the power and responsibility we have in creating our life experience. Her encouragement to reflect on how we can consciously use our energy and intention to shape our reality is memorable, emphasizing the power of the human mind and our connection to a broader universe.

One of the topics that most intrigued Dolores was the nature of the soul and parallel realities, raising intriguing questions about our existence and life choices. For her, we are part of an "Oversoul," a Higher Self, which divides into multiple fragments to simultaneously experience different lives. Every choice we make in the current life is just one of the infinite possibilities that our soul explores.

Also, very interesting in her work is the idea of people who are commonly considered "crazy" and confined to psychiatric institutions. For her, many of these people may actually have a greater awareness and connection to different realities. She mentioned the redefinition of schizophrenia in modern psychiatry, emphasizing that many people who hear voices might simply be in contact with other dimensions or aspects of themselves in parallel lives.

Our limited understanding of reality often leads us to misunderstand and isolate those who perceive dimensions different from our own. This suggests that many people considered mentally unstable may actually be more "connected" than we think. Her observation on this aspect highlighted the complexity of the human mind and the vastness of soul experiences, encouraging her readers to consider perspectives beyond the boundaries of their daily understanding.

For example, she also talked about the thin veil that separates different realities and how the use of substances like drugs can inadvertently open it, allowing access to dimensions other than the usual one. She warned about the dangers of this practice, emphasizing how it can confuse and destabilize the mind.

Important for Dolores is also the concept of the different personalities and incarnations that a soul can simultaneously explore. Although we are only aware of the current personality, there are other incarnations of our soul living parallel experiences.

Every experience, even negative ones like childhood abuse, are choices made by the soul to learn and grow. Central in her teachings is the importance of forgiveness and letting go of these experiences once the lessons they bring are understood. Traumatic experiences, such as childhood abuse, can be lessons in survival and resilience. She suggested that we are experiencing these difficult lessons because we are in a phase of expanding our awareness and abilities.

Dolores Cannon has made us understand through her enlightening books that advanced metaphysical knowledge, once reserved for a few initiates, is becoming accessible to a wider audience. These ancient and powerful pieces of information, once limited to mystery schools, are now coming to light for the general public, which appears ready to receive them.

Another important concept that Dolores Cannon wanted to emphasize is the importance of communicating with one's own body, emphasizing that every cell and organ represents an entire universe. To underline this important point, she cited the case of a doctor who published a book on this subject after running a hospital for 45 years, challenging the norms of traditional medicine, which tends to label people with unconventional perceptions as pathological.

From the work of this great woman, we learn the importance of considering life as a continuous learning process, where after "graduating" from Earth School, many more adventures and knowledge await us in other realms of existence.

We close this section by remembering how Dolores Cannon viewed the future: it is never set in stone and subject to countless probabilities and possibilities depending on individual choices. Her stance emphasizes the importance of personal action and the ability to influence one's own life path.

THE NEW EARTH: A VIBRATIONAL SHIFT

The concept of the "New Earth" conceived by Dolores Cannon represents a significant evolutionary leap, not only for the planet but also for humanity. According to her hypothesis, this phenomenon involves a profound transformation of the vibrations and frequencies of the planet, resulting in impacts on the reality in which we live. Here is a detailed description of this concept, summarized in its key points.

1. **Planetary Evolution**: Cannon viewed Earth as a living being evolving independently of human will. The New Earth represents a phase in this evolutionary process in which the planet elevates to a higher state of consciousness and frequency.

2. **Transition of Frequencies**: The transition to the New Earth is not a physical event but a vibrational one. It involves an increase in the energetic frequencies of the Earth, which influences the environment, human life, and consciousness.

3. **Impact on Human Beings**: This change requires that humanity also adapts. Humans must raise their vibrations to remain in harmony with the planet. This includes changes at both the levels of consciousness and the physical.

Human Role in Evolution

1. **DNA Transformation**: Cannon argued that to adapt to the New Earth, human DNA must undergo a change. This could manifest as new psychic abilities, greater empathy, and deeper awareness.

2. **Shift in Consciousness**: The transition to the New Earth is also an inner journey that requires a new understanding of reality. It implies the development of a more unified and collaboration-oriented consciousness rather than competition.

3. **Importance of Choice and Intention**: Cannon emphasized the power of individual choices and intentions in contributing to this process. Each person has a role to play in creating the New Earth through their actions and spiritual development.

Challenges and Opportunities

1. **Avoiding Historical Mistakes**: A crucial aspect of the transition to the New Earth is avoiding the mistakes that led to the downfall of previous civilizations, such as Atlantis. Cannon warned against the abuse of power and greed that could hinder this progress.

2. **Responsible Use of Technology**: Cannon's concerns also included the ethical use of technology. She cautioned that practices like genetic manipulation and the creation of human-animal hybrids could have unforeseen and harmful consequences.

Grid Keepers and Children of the New Era

1. **Grid Keepers**: According to Cannon, there exists a group of souls called "grid keepers" whose task is to maintain and repair the energetic grids of the Earth. These individuals often operate unconsciously, contributing to the evolutionary process during sleep or in alternative dimensions.

2. **Children of the New Era**: Cannon also spoke of new waves of souls, such as indigo, crystal, and rainbow children, who incarnate with a consciousness already aligned with the frequencies of the New Earth. These children represent the future and bring new ideas and ways of being.

Transition and Preparation

1. **Physical and Spiritual Adaptation**: Preparation for the

New Earth includes changes in diet and lifestyle, favoring lighter and natural foods, as well as inner work to release karma and fear.

2. **Continuous Journey**: Cannon emphasized that the transition to the New Earth is an ongoing process, not a single event. It is a journey that requires continuous awareness, spiritual growth, and personal commitment.

In summary, Dolores Cannon's concept of the New Earth describes a profound shift in the consciousness and physical reality of the planet and humanity. It is an evolutionary process that requires both internal and external transformation, marking a significant step in human evolution.

Dolores Cannon investigated an epochal transition in which the Earth and humanity advance toward a new reality characterized by a mutation of vibrations and frequencies. This unique phenomenon in the history of universes has captured the attention of beings located on other planets and dimensions, eager to observe how humanity will handle this crucial evolutionary challenge.

She noted that Earth, conceived as a living entity in constant evolution, is moving independently of human presence. To keep pace with these changes, humanity is called to evolve, transforming their bodies to adapt to the planet's changes.

However, through her in-depth research, Dolores Cannon identified a concerning pattern in human evolution: the repetition of historical mistakes similar to those that led to the downfall of advanced civilizations like Atlantis. According to her analysis, these civilizations had reached a remarkable level of knowledge and development but were ruined by human greed and lust for power. She also highlighted on multiple occasions the dangers associated with modern technological research, such as genetic manipulation and the development of human-animal hybrids, practices that risk violating natural laws and leading to unforeseen and potentially disastrous consequences.

Her distinction between cloning, a subject of extensive ethical debate, and the fusion of human and animal DNA is a crucial point in her research. While cloning raises complex moral questions, the crossing of human and animal DNA raises more immediate and serious concerns, given the unpredictability of its effects and the potential to create new life forms with unknown ethical and practical implications. It's essential to keep in mind that all these dangers could hinder humanity's transition to the new Earth, making it the responsibility of each of us to engage at the social and civil levels to combat these dangerous distortions.

Even the existence of subterranean civilizations, which would have survived ancient catastrophes like the one

47

that struck Atlantis, has been the subject of study by Dolores, who described these communities as technically advanced and self-sufficient, living in well-organized cities and isolated from the challenges of the Earth's surface. These civilizations, according to her research, exist in parallel to our world but remain detached and protected from the issues we face on the surface.

We have already seen that one of the most intriguing aspects of Cannon's research concerns the so-called "grid keepers." These ten thousand souls, already present and active on Earth, are engaged in a crucial task of adapting the Earth's energetic grids, primarily operating during sleep, shifting into other dimensions. These souls, although they have a physical presence on our planet, operate beyond the limits of the material world. Cannon collected testimonies from these souls, including one who lived during the collapse of Atlantis and worked on the energetic grids before the disappearance of that civilization.

Regarding the Sapphire Children, the researcher did not exclude the possibility that they may represent another wave of souls, similar to the Indigo or Crystal children. She also identified the arrival of Rainbow children, a more recent group of souls with a specific and vital role in the global transformation process.

She left us with advice to facilitate the transition to the New Earth. For her, it is essential to follow a lighter diet based on raw and unprocessed foods to ease this transition.

THE THREE WAVES OF VOLUNTEERS

In a chapter steeped in mystery and deep historical insight, Dolores Cannon unveiled a hidden narrative woven into the very fabric of human existence. Through her inquisitive lens, the Ancients emerged: majestic and almost mythological beings, silent custodians of our planet, Earth. According to Dolores's findings, these Ancients were not mere observers but actual architects of life, playing a crucial role in its initial creation.

At the heart of her narrative, Dolores took the reader on a journey through the ages, painting a story that unfolded and intertwined over millennia. The Ancients, in their wisdom and power, had sown the seeds of life on Earth, overseeing the development of humanity with an almost parental care. Yet, they were bound by an immutable and universal law: the law of non-interference. This law compelled them to remain observers, preventing direct intervention in human affairs, a choice that reflected their respect for human free will.

Despite the restrictions imposed by this cosmic law, the Ancients managed to exert a subtle but significant influence on human history. Dolores described how they did so, for example, through bearers of culture, legendary figures who emerged in every civilization, bringing gifts of knowledge and innovation. These beings, who walked among humans as celestial messengers, taught the art of agriculture, gave the gift of fire, and imparted wisdom that would be essential for human progress.

Dolores's narrative was not only an exploration of the past but also a reflection on the present and future of humanity. She revealed how, throughout history, humanity had often misused these precious gifts, turning them into instruments of destruction rather than growth and prosperity. The Ancients, with a mixture of disappointment and hope, watched from afar, eager for their "earthly children" to learn to use knowledge and technology wisely.

In summary, through her narrative, Dolores Cannon offered a unique and fascinating vision of human history, a storytelling that connected the ancient to the modern and opened new perspectives on our understanding of the universe and our place within it. It was a story that extended beyond time and space, touching the core of our existence and challenging our understanding of what it means to be human.

Dolores examined the intrinsic dualism of humanity, which often distorted these gifts, turning them into instruments of destruction rather than progress. The Ancients, detached yet affectionate observers, could do nothing but hope that humanity would learn from its choices.

During her years of in-depth research, Dolores Cannon

had uncovered and narrated a story that intertwined the fate of humanity with enigmatic entities known as the Ancients. Despite their hands being tied by this universal law of non-interference, the Ancients had, as we have seen, found ways to influence human history more subtly.

A significant shift in their attitude had occurred with the conclusion of World War II. The use of atomic bombs marked a critical turning point, drawing the concerned attention of the Ancients to an unprecedented level. Worried about humanity's potential for self-destruction and its negative influence on the entire universe, they began to observe more closely, although their respect for human free will prevented them from intervening directly.

Dolores Cannon, in her study filled with manuscripts and historical memories, had reconstructed an important chapter in contemporary history, linked to the emergence of UFO phenomena in the late 1940s and early 1950s. During this period, marked by the end of World War II, UFO sightings had exponentially increased, and Dolores had started to investigate why this sudden proliferation was happening.

According to her research, atomic energy, a powerful and dangerous force, was not yet supposed to be in our temporal path. It was an energy destined to be discovered in the future and used for positive purposes, but humanity, by turning it into a destructive weapon, had drawn the Ancients' attention, who were concerned about the planet's fate.

The use of atomic bombs represented a critical turning point. The Ancients, concerned that humanity might self-destruct and negatively affect the entire universe, considered the possibility of intervention. However, out of respect for human free will, they were forced to seek alternative solutions.

Dolores discovered that the Ancients had devised a clever plan: they had issued a call for volunteers throughout the solar system and beyond, inviting beings from different civilizations to incarnate on Earth to positively influence its destiny. According to her account, this was the foundation of what she called the "three waves of volunteers."

The first wave of volunteers, as Dolores had discovered in her past life regression sessions, consisted of souls who had never experienced earthly violence or accumulated karma. They were "pure" souls who began incarnating shortly after the release of atomic bombs. These individuals, according to Dolores, were often strangers to earthly life, originating from other planets, spacecraft, dimensions, or even as beings of light.

Dolores noted that instead of reliving typical earthly past lives, these people, during regression sessions, returned to the Source or to extraterrestrial experiences, demonstrating that they had never lived on Earth before.

This change in her regression sessions marked a turning point for her in understanding human evolution and the role of extraterrestrials in our development.

In a fascinating chapter of her research, Dolores Cannon delved into a phenomenon she described with the evocative term "the three waves of volunteers." This part of her work highlighted a series of testimonies that diverged from typical past earthly lives, revealing extraterrestrial or dimensional origins of the subjects involved. These individuals, as described by Dolores, had no previous earthly incarnations and had responded to a universal call to assist Earth.

Dolores recounted how these souls, initially existing in states of pure happiness and innocence, were moved by the will to help humanity. However, once incarnated, they confronted the density and complexity of human emotions, often feeling alien and ill-suited to this world. Their earthly existence was characterized by a sense of estrangement, a desire to "go home," and an intense aversion to earthly violence and negativity.

These volunteers, in response to the call, decided to incarnate on Earth. Their stories, as told by Dolores, were poignant: when they arrived here, they found themselves disoriented and overwhelmed by the emotional and physical density of our world. Often, these individuals felt a deep sense of disconnection and a burning desire to return "home," a place they couldn't define but felt was not Earth.

These stories were, for Dolores, vivid examples of the complexity of human existence. It was not just an earthly journey but a fragment of a much larger cosmic mosaic. Reflecting on these testimonies, Dolores invited us to consider humanity not only as an isolated species but as an integral part of a vast and intricate universe of life and consciousness.

Dolores's findings focused particularly on the first wave of these volunteers, individuals who often felt isolated and misunderstood in a world that did not meet their expectations. These individuals, despite possessing great abilities and sensitivity, found it challenging to adapt to life on Earth, often struggling to cope with daily reality.

In one of the cases documented by Dolores, a person from the first wave, who had contacted her, had shown an unusual ability to adapt to earthly life. Dolores interpreted this case as a signal that perhaps some volunteers had been better prepared or advised before their incarnation, or that some souls had arrived ahead of the true wave of volunteers, acting as "explorers" of an unknown human experience.

According to Cannon, the waves of volunteers are not an alien invasion but a subtle process of inner conditioning. Their main mission was and is to raise the vibrations and frequencies of Earth, a process planned for a long time but accelerated by the post-World War II nuclear crisis.

Many of these volunteers, coming from different worlds

and dimensions, responded to the call to assist Earth. However, as mentioned earlier, Dolores observed that often these individuals, once incarnated, felt disoriented and lost, struggling to adapt to the emotional and energetic density of earthly life. This internal struggle emerged in numerous cases studied by Dolores, where the volunteers expressed a desire to return "home," even though they couldn't define that concept.

The second wave of volunteers, younger and seemingly more adaptable, consisted of individuals who served as energy channels. These individuals often led isolated lives, working from home or avoiding intense social interactions. Their solitary presence in public places, such as malls or shops, was sufficient to radiate positive energy and love, thus influencing anyone they came into contact with.

Understanding and accepting their role, according to Dolores, was key for these volunteers. They didn't need to take specific actions; their mere existence, their "being," was enough to positively influence the surrounding environment and contribute to Earth's ascension. This perspective offered an optimistic and powerful view of human potential within a complex and interconnected universe.

During her research, as we have seen, Dolores Cannon explored the influence of family relationships on karma accumulation. She discovered that closer relationships, such as those with spouses, children, tended to accumulate more karma due to their intimacy and emotional intensity. This discovery led to the understanding that many of the volunteers from the first two waves consciously or unconsciously chose not to have children to avoid creating deep karmic bonds that could hinder their mission on Earth.

The difficulties of adapting energies between mother and child were particularly evident. Some women from the first wave experienced complicated pregnancies, with difficulties in conceiving or carrying a pregnancy to term. Some had to endure long hospitalizations or miscarriages, highlighting the challenges of energy adaptation.

Dolores found that the problems were often due to significant energy differences between mother and child, especially when the mother had never had earthly experiences before that life. In some cases, it was observed that only a portion of the soul's energy was transmitted to the fetus to facilitate the birth process. Many people from the first wave later reported having mothers who had lost a child before them.

For example, a young girl exhibited symptoms resembling epileptic seizures, but doctors couldn't diagnose epilepsy. Dolores's research revealed that these problems were due to energy imbalances caused by the amplification of energy. She suggested that these individuals might require a reduction in energy intensity to alleviate the imbalances.

The third wave, known as the "new children," included individuals with DNA already adapted to the new energies, setting them apart from their predecessors. These children, often identified as "indigo children," arrived with modified DNA, ready to face the challenges of the new world. Dolores Cannon emphasized that these children represent a significant gift to the world and have the potential to bring about meaningful changes.

She observed that these children learn at an incredibly rapid pace, often leading to feelings of boredom and frustration in traditional educational settings. Teachers frequently find themselves dealing with the restlessness of these children, who, with their intuitive grasp of complex concepts like mathematics, simply respond with "I know" when questioned about their answers.

Dolores stressed the need to challenge these children in unconventional ways, suggesting hands-on activities like disassembling and reassembling objects to stimulate their minds. She emphasized that, despite their extraordinary intelligence and sensitivity, these children still require appropriate parental guidance.

She also discovered that many of these children have modified DNA, indicating their unique nature and the role they are destined to play in the world. These DNA changes, according to some research, could lead to a human race less susceptible to diseases. She cautioned against using drugs like Ritalin for these children, as it could interfere with their particular brainwaves.

We already know that Dolores delved deeply into the topics of reincarnation and the evolution of the soul. She did so to explain that we are more than what appears in a single physical body; we have existed in many forms on various planets and dimensions. This understanding leads us to realize that there is no clear separation between "us" and "others," including extraterrestrials. We are all connected in a continuum of experiences and lessons learned through various lifetimes. This is undoubtedly a revolutionary concept that emerges from the research of this extraordinary researcher.

In her research, Dolores Cannon also explored the relationship between humans and extraterrestrials, discovering a deep and positive connection. According to her findings, ETs are beings guided by love and a desire to help, contrasting with the common perception of fear and distrust. Dolores argued that fear is an intrinsic emotion to the earthly dimension but is also one that humanity is shedding during this period of great change.

She highlighted the need to overcome fear for personal evolution, emphasizing that fear is a choice, not a necessity. She spoke of the uniqueness of each human being, who is much more than a physical body in a specific time and space. Throughout existence, each of us has taken various physical forms on different planets and dimensions, experiencing a wide range of experiences.

Her research revealed that the true essence of a human being transcends the boundaries of physical form. We are all interconnected in a cosmic fabric that goes beyond the concepts of time and space. This web of lives unites us with ETs, all beings of light, and every form of life in other dimensions. In this context, the fear of extraterrestrials and other life forms becomes irrelevant, as we are all part of one grand universal design. Her vision was that of a world without divisions and fear, where we recognize that "we are all one."

REVELATIONS ABOUT ATLANTIS: THE RISE AND FALL OF AN ANCIENT CIVILIZATION

Through regression hypnosis sessions conducted by Dolores Cannon, many details about the history of Atlantis emerged. By collecting testimonies from patients who, under hypnosis, described past lives lived in Atlantis, Dolores gathered a wealth of intriguing information that she later shared through her lectures and writings. According to the gathered testimonies, in a remote period of history, the civilization of Atlantis had reached an advanced level of development, surpassing our current technological and spiritual understanding. This civilization, spread worldwide, wasn't limited to a single island but comprised a network of magnificent cities and diverse communities. The inhabitants of these cities had developed extraordinary mental abilities that allowed them to manipulate matter, create impressive structures like pyramids, and even control their physical well-being, eliminating diseases and aging.

However, as time passed, they began to experiment in ways that went against the laws of nature. Using crystals and other technologies, they started conducting experiments to hybridize humans and animals, creating beings for servile purposes or mere curiosity. These creatures, often unable to reproduce, later became the mythological figures we know as centaurs, minotaurs, and other hybrid creatures, whose stories survived in the legends of ancient Greece and Rome.

The misuse of these powerful abilities led Atlantis to a point of great crisis. In particular, the improper use of crystals to generate excessive energy directed towards the Earth's core began to destabilize the region. Their unrestrained experiments, aimed at testing the limits of what was possible without considering the consequences, ultimately led to the inevitable destruction of the Atlantean civilization.

Interestingly, there is a connection, as discovered by Dolores, between the disappearance of Atlantis and the Bermuda Triangle. Her research revealed that in the area where the Bermuda Triangle is now located, there once existed an Atlantean temple that housed a sort of time machine capable of traveling through different dimensions. With the cataclysm that swallowed Atlantis, this machine was damaged and remained on the ocean floor, still emitting irregular energy waves. This phenomenon would be the cause of the unexplained events associated with the Bermuda Triangle: the disappearance of ships and aircraft, temporal anomalies, and other unsolved mysteries.

This narrative, the result of centuries of transmissions and speculative theories, transports us to a time when the line between science and myth was still undefined, and where human civilization, in its highest aspirations, touched the boundaries of the unknown, only to disappear, leaving echoes in history and myth.

In those times, the existence of advanced civilizations like Atlantis was characterized by an intense use of mental abilities. However, these civilizations were not isolated; many other highly developed societies were lost for similar reasons. Their downfall was often linked to the abuse of power and the desire for dominance (sound familiar to our own times?). A surprising revelation emerged from Dolores Cannon's regression hypnosis sessions regarding a group of women who lived in one of these ancient and advanced civilizations. These women, gathered in a temple, sought to counter destructive energies by performing ceremonies to repair an apocalyptic damage: an ozone hole, caused by dangerous manipulations, which allowed solar rays to penetrate and scorch vast territories. Despite their efforts, the disaster was inevitable. The area they tried to save turned into the Sahara Desert, once a tropical paradise.

These stories that Dolores shared and that emerged from her regression hypnosis sessions with patients who had lived in those ancient times, in those civilizations, suggest a cyclical nature in human history: the attainment of technological and spiritual heights followed by self-destruction due to the abuse of power. It's as if humanity, over the ages, had "blown a mental fuse," losing the ability to fully utilize their mental capabilities. Such a loss was seen as a safety measure to prevent further abuse, as explained by Dolores Cannon's guides who communicated with her through the patients in hypnosis.

Ancient tales, like that of the Tower of Babel in the Bible, are interpreted as metaphors for these abuses of power, just as the biblical narrative of the confusion of languages is seen as a simplification of a more complex event related to the abuse of human abilities.

In the current context, according to Dolores' deductions from her studies, she stated that humanity is slowly regaining these lost abilities. There is indeed a growing interest in alternative healing practices and a renewed exploration of psychic abilities. Many are turning to sound therapy, light therapy, and other forms of healing. This resurgence is particularly evident in children, who seem to be natural carriers of these renewed capabilities.

In this emerging scenario, the concept of the "New Earth" takes on a particular significance. Rather than cyclically repeating past mistakes, humanity is approaching a turning point, where the lessons learned from lost civilizations can guide humanity toward a more conscious and harmonious future, utilizing their innate abilities. In this new era, humanity might be able to handle power with wisdom and responsibility, paving the way for an entirely new level of existence.

During one of her lectures, the theme of the "New Earth"

was presented with great enthusiasm. She explained how the planet was entering a period of significant transition, a moment of metamorphosis that the Earth and humanity had never experienced before in the history of galaxies and universes. According to the shared information, the Earth was entering a completely new dimension, with rapidly changing frequencies and vibrations. This transition was compared to what was foretold in the Mayan prophecies, predicting a great change in 2012. Regarding the mysterious disappearance of this South American civilization, Dolores explained that the Maya, as a civilization, had managed to mass-transition to another dimension, leaving the physical world behind. Their disappearance and the end of their calendar were interpreted as an omen for a future event, when the entire planet would undergo a similar leap, akin to what they had already experienced.

And Cannon emphasized that the entire universe was watching this unique phenomenon. Earth, described as an entity emitting a distinct and recordable sound, was changing its tone, an indicator that something extraordinary was happening. These transformations are not just external; they also influence humans on a physical level. Many people report even today, anomalies in their bodies, such as heart problems or dizziness, that doctors cannot explain. These phenomena are interpreted as reactions to the changing energies and frequencies of the planet.

This transition process towards the New Earth was described as necessarily gradual. A too rapid change would have been unsustainable for physical bodies. Therefore, adaptation occurs in small steps, with periods of adjustment between one change and another.

The New Earth is presented, in Dolores Cannon's work, as a magnificent and beautiful world, radically different from the current one. Through this process, humanity and the planet can overcome old destructive and karmic patterns, moving towards a more harmonious and conscious existence. This vision undoubtedly offers a perspective of hope and rebirth, an invitation to embark on a collective journey toward a renewed reality full of possibilities.

Also, very interesting is the question of those who would be "left behind" during the transition to the New Earth. Dolores explained very clearly that, although this may seem harsh, the process is actually fair: every individual had the same opportunities to adapt and change. However, those who couldn't quickly adjust their vibrational frequency would remain with the old Earth. This choice, although it might appear challenging, was a natural step in individual evolution.

Those who remain with the old Earth will continue to live in a world marked by violence and negativity and will have to work on their karma. Once that life is over, they will no longer return to Earth but will be sent to other planets still trapped in negativity and violence. And

Dolores emphasized that this was not a cruel process but a normal passage through different levels of spiritual development.

It's also important to understand how she explained how the human body was adapting to these changes. She predicted that people's dietary habits would change, preferring lighter foods and gradually transitioning to consuming only liquids, in line with the body's need to become lighter to adapt to the new vibrational frequency. This process of lightening would occur naturally, without conscious effort.

In this context, an anecdote comes to mind where Dolores spoke of a vision had by Annie Kirkwood, author of "Mary's Message to the World." In the vision, she saw the Earth dividing into two, like a cell splitting. In one of the "Earths," people expressed joy at having made the transition, while in the other, those who had not undergone the transition continued to live unconsciously, as if nothing had changed.

Dolores also suggested that, to facilitate the transfer of entire populations to the New Earth, people might be put into a kind of suspended state. When they woke up, they would think it was the next day when, in reality, weeks had passed. This process had already been used in the past for cosmic interventions, such as repairing the sun. But what exactly is this sun repair? According to the information obtained from her sessions, there would have been a time in history (not specified and outside of conventional scientific context) when the sun needed to be "repaired" or adjusted.

In this context, there would have been a cosmic-scale intervention conducted by advanced beings or unknown forces to make changes or corrections to the sun. During this process, according to Cannon, the Earth's population would have been put into a kind of "suspended animation" to prevent them from noticing these cosmic changes.

But to conclude this section, it's important to remember how Dolores always emphasized that love is the key to further elevating the vibrations and frequencies of individuals, moving them away from violence and promoting harmony. This teaching, already espoused by great historical figures such as Gandhi and Jesus, is seen as fundamental in the transition to the New Earth. Love, in conclusion, can be the driving force for profound and positive change for all of humanity.

ASTRAL TRAVEL

Dolores Cannon, throughout her prolific career as a hypnotherapist and writer, explored a wide range of phenomena related to human consciousness, including astral projections. According to her, astral projections occur when consciousness, or what some might call the soul or spirit, temporarily leaves the physical body to travel to other dimensions or realities. Dolores viewed this phenomenon not as a fantasy or dream but as a genuine journey of a part of ourselves into worlds and existential planes beyond our ordinary understanding.

In her numerous books and interviews, she described in detail how many of her clients, through regression hypnosis sessions, revealed experiences of astral projections. These narratives often included vivid and consistent details about places and entities encountered during these journeys, which she interpreted as evidence of the existence of parallel realities and different levels of existence.

Dolores Cannon emphasized that astral projections can occur both consciously and unconsciously. Some individuals can learn to induce these astral travels through meditation or relaxation techniques, while others may experience them spontaneously, often during sleep. She repeatedly stressed that during these experiences, we are always connected to our physical body by a "silver cord," a sort of energetic link that allows us to return to our physical state at any time.

In her interpretation, she saw astral projections not only as curious phenomena but as opportunities for learning and spiritual growth. She theorized that during these astral journeys, we can gain profound insights, encounter spiritual guides, and even resolve unresolved issues or traumas from our past. Furthermore, she believed that these experiences could offer a glimpse of the afterlife and past existences, expanding our understanding of life, death, and the journey of the soul.

Through her work, Dolores Cannon contributed to bringing the concept of astral projections to the attention of a wider audience, sparking increasing interest in these mysterious journeys of consciousness. Her research and theories continue to influence and inspire those who explore the boundaries of human existence and seek answers to life's profound mysteries.

Now, let's translate the story of a specific astral projection experience reported by one of her patients:

During a session, Dolores's patient was guided into a state of deep relaxation, entering a phase of regression hypnosis. In this state, he began to describe an experience in which he felt his consciousness detaching from his physical body. He described this sensation as liberating and peaceful, a sort of levitation that carried him above his physical form.

The patient then narrated traveling through a luminous

tunnel, at the end of which he reached a place he perceived as profoundly familiar yet different from anything he had ever experienced on Earth. In this place, he encountered beings of light that he perceived as spiritual guides. These entities did not communicate verbally but transmitted knowledge and understanding through a form of telepathic communication.

One of the most astonishing revelations during this astral journey was the vision of the patient's past lives. He saw himself in various historical eras and cultural contexts, gaining a new perspective on his current existence. This experience provided deep insights into the cyclical nature of life and reincarnation, as well as the connections between his past experiences and his current life.

Additionally, the patient described receiving spiritual healing and understanding from these guides, who worked with him to resolve unresolved traumas and issues, both from his current life and past ones. He perceived this experience as a form of spiritual therapy that had a profound and lasting impact on his emotional and spiritual well-being.

Upon returning to his physical body, the patient reported a sense of renewal and deeper understanding of his life and existential purpose. This astral projection experience, as recounted by Dolores Cannon, illustrates the potential of out-of-body experiences to provide profound spiritual healing and understanding, a recurring theme in Cannon's work.

DOLORES CANNON'S RESPONSES

(Directly transcribed from real conferences held by Dolores Cannon)

What is the subconscious?

"I have been doing this work for 45 years, and over time, I developed my own technique. Because 45 years ago, nobody was doing what I was doing. There were no books or information to teach you how to do it. I had to create my own technique. And gradually, over time, I discovered new things that no one else had discovered.

After a while, a kind of force began to emerge during the sessions. Now I know it's the greatest force in the universe. There is nothing greater. It possesses absolute power. It can answer any question, and it can even provide an immediate cure for anything.

This is what I work with now. I didn't know what to call it. At first, I called it the subconscious because I didn't have another term to define it. And they told me: 'It doesn't matter because we don't have a name anyway. We will work with you.'

Some people say we communicate with the Higher Self, the Higher Soul, the Higher Consciousness. Some call it Universal Consciousness. All these names signify something immense, and we found a way to communicate with it. So, I call it the Subconscious.

My students call it the SC. It has absolute power. And it's also unconditional love. It's a joy to work with and see the miracles it can perform. It enters the person and heals them instantly. It's wonderful to see. And it's the energy I constantly work with.

It's beautiful and very, very effective. I encourage anyone interested in Quantum Hypnosis Regression to take the training course. The training is available online. You will find it on my website www.dolorescannon.com."

What is the QHHT technique?

"I began teaching in 2002, and initially, I only did past life regression and the Higher Consciousness part. I hadn't yet discovered or practiced many treatments. So, at that time, the course was called 'Advanced Past Life Regression' only, but over time, we understood the power of the technique and what we could do with it.

Many students began to say: 'You know, this name doesn't do it justice. It's much more than that, we think you should change it.' So, a few years ago, we decided to change it to 'Quantum Healing Hypnosis Technique' because that's what it really is. It's quantum. It's so vast and important.

So now we call it Quantum Healing Hypnosis Technique because it goes beyond simple regression. That's what we call it now. And it's the technique I've been teaching since 2002. It's been 12 years. I encourage anyone interested in the Quantum Healing Hypnosis Technique to take the training course. The training is available online. You will find it on my website www.dolorescannon.com."

What does it feel like to go into trance?

"Many of my clients ask me what it will feel like when they go into trance and experience a past life regression. I tell them it's similar to taking a nap. Often, they are nervous and worried, and I ask them if they enjoy taking a nap. It's just that easy and simple.

It's just like taking a nap. And they will see images from past lives. So, I tell them they have the easiest role. They just need to relax and look at the beautiful images and tell me what they see. Mine is the most challenging role; I have to ask the right questions to find the answers and connect them.

The role of the hypnotized subject is very easy and straightforward. What many people don't know is that they are hypnotized most of the time. It's impossible for anyone to stay completely awake all the time. It's a completely normal, natural, and safe aspect of human behavior.

All we do is utilize this normal state in therapy. I encourage anyone interested in Quantum Regression

Hypnosis to take advantage of the training course. The training is now available online. You will find it on my website DoloresCannon.com."

What does it feel like to revisit one's past lives?

"With this technique, the first thing we do is visit a client's past life. Many answers will be there, as some of the answers to this current life go back to past lives. Whether it's illnesses, phobias, or something else. So, past life is the beginning, it's the tip of the iceberg. Because we go much further, but entering a past life is very simple. And we do it with Quantum Healing Hypnosis Technique. But I never know where the person will go. That's what's fun because it's always surprising; you never know in advance what the connections are.

But it will always be the right time and place to explain what's happening in their current life. That's how they find the answers. But past life is just the beginning. Then, we call upon that great force I work with. From there, all the healing and answers come, and all the work is done. Past life is easy. You just have to go into a trance and go into the past and find the most suitable life for you at that moment. I encourage anyone interested in Quantum Healing Hypnosis Technique to take the training course. The training is now available online. You'll find it on my website www.dolorescannon.com."

Can extraterrestrials be contacted with QHHT?

"It's not exactly the same because it's not about healing. For 27 years, I have been investigating UFOs and have found all the answers to questions that anyone might have. I've written four books on the subject. It is possible to contact extraterrestrials using the Quantum Healing Hypnosis Technique, using the first part of regression into past lives.

Most of the time, when they enter a past life, they end up in a place where they were extraterrestrials, on a spaceship, or on another planet. You never know where they will go, but what emerges is what they need to know. Initially, with 'The Custodians' and the other books, I focused on a single story, so we had multiple sessions with the same person to get the entire story.

That's what hypnosis was for me until 20 years ago when I discovered this other way of working with the Higher Consciousness. I still work slightly differently from other hypnotherapists. I encourage anyone interested in Quantum Healing Hypnosis Technique to participate in the training course. The training is available online. You'll find it on my website www.dolorescannon.com."

What is your favorite experience with QHHT?

"It's always a unique experience for the client, but for me, it happens every day in my office, so it's quite challenging to describe one, as it's case by case. As soon as they leave, I forget everything about the session because it's already the next client's turn. But I've seen human bodies heal and recover completely.

I've had patients who were supposed to undergo surgeries and left my office without needing them anymore. They came in with issues, and during the session, they could feel bones moving and cracking. I would ask their Higher Self, 'What are you doing?' And they would reply, 'We are realigning the vertebrae and putting everything back in place.' What they did didn't cause any pain to the patient. It was energetic work, white light energy. Like electrical currents. But they said they were putting everything back in place. The client could feel it, even the sound of bones cracking on their mp3 player. I've seen people with crooked bones or liver cirrhosis.

I've witnessed complete remissions; everything got resolved. I've seen things that are absolutely impossible to achieve. One day, a woman came to me and said she was dying. She was in palliative care but still came, with a walker and a friend accompanying her. She brought a big oxygen therapy machine with her, connected to an oxygen tank by a hose.

We placed it in another room during the hypnosis, but it was still connected. During the session, her Higher Self started working on her. It went deep into her lungs and reinflated the lower lobes. The lower lobes of her lungs.

Then it cleared all impurities in other parts of the lungs, and it happens quickly; it doesn't take much time to do all this. While we were doing all this, there was a power outage in the building. I wasn't worried because the session was recorded on a digital recorder, but there was no electricity anymore. The oxygen machine was in the other room and started making a terrible screeching noise.

So, I asked them, 'What's that?' And they replied, 'It's her respiratory device, turn it off; she doesn't need it anymore!' I turned it off, and indeed, she didn't need it for the entire time she lived. And when we were done, it was a real miracle. She wasn't the same person who had entered my office. Her friend came to pick her up, and she left without any issues. When she went back to the doctor, she said, 'Get a chest X-ray for me and check it, especially the lower lobes.' She had the X-ray, and the doctor said, 'What? There's nothing; your lungs are healthy.'

That's one of the success stories I love to share because two months later, we were organizing our Transformation Conference. She came to the conference, running all over the hallways and back in the hotel and the auditorium, laughing and having a wonderful time. She was unrecognizable, no longer the same person. In the end, she trained in my technique. She told everyone that thanks to this, she had achieved incredible results that doctors couldn't explain. One thing I like: when she went back home, we received a postcard from one of her daughters that said, 'Thank you for giving us our mother back.'"

We had seen her a few months before at that conference, and her daughters told us she had a new grandchild, adding, 'She could have never lived to see it now without the work you did.' This is one of my greatest satisfactions. Seeing these people's lives completely reinvented. And now, in turn, she helps others through Quantum Healing Hypnosis Technique. That's where I find my happiness and fulfillment. Teaching. Discovering and teaching, and having the desire for the world to know how powerful your mind is.

Why should I become a QHHT practitioner?

"For me, Quantum Healing Hypnosis Technique is the most effective healing method that exists. When I speak to clients, they come with all kinds of illnesses, disorders, and problems. In most cases, when they arrive at my office, they are in critical condition. Doctors have given up on helping them.

They are referred to palliative care or simply told, 'Go home and prepare to die; it's all we can do.' So, I see very sick people coming to my office seeking help. The first thing I tell these people when they enter is: 'No one should ever be sick. You should never suffer or have any symptoms.' Because the human body is a miraculous machine designed to heal itself without external interference.

Then I tell the person: 'You got sick on your own.' And many of them respond, 'How so? I don't want to be sick.' But if the human mind is powerful enough to make you sick, it's also powerful enough to heal you. You just have to discover why you did it to yourself. Often, it's an awakening when they start saying, 'I did this?' 'I did this? I did this.' When they start saying, 'Oh! So, it's not anyone else's fault.' There are no victims. 'I created this. If I created it, I can also undo it.' That's the power of the mind. It's with this power that I work constantly.

To understand the person, we find answers to all the questions in past lives and in the part where we communicate with the Higher Consciousness. This explains exactly where the illness comes from. Of course, the location of the illness also says a lot about its message. The body is an extraordinary messenger; it always conveys the same messages. So, we've learned what back problems mean, what it means if your legs or hips, or your stomach, or liver, or kidneys are affected.

We know what these messages mean and what the body is trying to communicate. Once you do this and continue on this path, healing is instantaneous because they finally understand. It's what I did. That's why Quantum Healing Hypnosis Technique is such a powerful tool. We work with doctors around the world who integrate this technique into their practice. Many of these doctors leave their profession and turn to natural and alternative medicines. It fits perfectly with what they do. It shows people the power of their minds.

You are not under anyone else's control but your own mind. You are not a victim. You have control over everything that happens in your life. If you don't like it, you can change it. People become aware of what they can do, and it's very powerful. We tell them that they are great and powerful beings. But they have forgotten. I invite anyone interested in Quantum Healing Hypnosis Technique to take advantage of the training. The training is now available online. You'll find it on my website www.dolorescannon.com."

What have you understood about Creation?

"Well, the idea is that nothing is real anyway, everything is energy, everything is an illusion. This building where you are right now didn't even exist until you collectively chose to come here tonight or today. Try to grasp this concept; I won't ask you to make sense of it because every time I talked about it, people said, 'It's like a Stephen King movie where nothing existed before they got there.' It's true; what you're doing is creating your own realities, and there... you've created a big group reality, and without this big group reality, this wouldn't exist. But it also shows you how powerful your mind is because everything you see, everything around you, everything in your life, you're creating and putting there to fill your world. So, it means you can create anything, nothing is impossible, you can change your life, you can manage anything in your life. I've been told that one of the biggest lessons you have to learn coming to Earth is how to manipulate energy. You can't graduate from Earth school until you learn how to manipulate energy. What does it mean? It means creating; you have to learn to create because your mind is so powerful. You can create anything, so every time you go somewhere, even when you return to your home, it gets recreated every time you enter. I wondered where it goes in the meantime; it's just space, it goes back into... whatever it is, but when these concepts started emerging, you know, it's a bit mind-boggling, but the audience of people really blew my mind, and wherever I go now, they say: tell us more about the background people, okay? It's creating, this is your movie, this is your performance, you are everything, life is in any case just a game, it's just a performance, it's just an illusion, you'll leave here with your brain really spinning, but I've heard people say that when they go through the experience of past lives, they look back and say, 'It was just a performance, I see all the actors on stage getting ready to play their parts, I see the actors backstage getting ready to go on stage and play their parts, it's just a performance, but when I was there... I took it so seriously, but now it's like the blink of an eye, so you are the producer, the director, and the actor of your own performance, you are also the scriptwriter but the script is not written, it's written as you go along, you see, you can change it anytime you want, we can feel trapped in thinking there's no way out, that this is all there is when you realize how powerful your mind is, you can create anything you want, that's the main goal of being alive, it's knowing, learning how to create, and now that the veil is lifting, we're entering this new Earth, we're going through the change, we're bringing all these abilities back, that's what you should learn to do."

What are parallel lives exactly?

"To keep it simple, at the beginning, everything is energy, everything. So, when you make a decision, you come to a crossroads in your life, you have to make a decision. Do I get married? Do I get divorced? Do I take this job? Do I go to this school? You're trying to make a decision about which path you want to take; we have these crossroads, and you know that in both cases you choose, your life will be different, right? Whether you marry this person or not, or if you get divorced, or if I choose this job, I should move, your life will be different, no matter which direction you take. So, you're trying to make a decision, and you put a lot of energy into making that decision, then in the end, you decide, okay, this is how I want to go. All right, what happens to the other alternative decision you could have taken? What happens to that? Its life is created, and another you is living that other

84

decision, and this can get a bit complicated for people. You're living this life, and you're focusing on the decision you made, but another you has branched off from here and is living that other life, and we shouldn't know it because it would be too complicated, that's what they say, you can't know everything. Imagine how complicated it would be if you knew about these other parts that all have these other experiences. I have clients who come to me and say, you know, I know I'm living another existence in another city, and I have another family there too, sometimes I spy on them, and they say it's possible, but you shouldn't do it because it would cause interference because the other reality is not aware of what's happening here. Now, I hope I've explained where I'm going with this; these are very complicated concepts, this is the simple explanation, it can get much more complicated if you split it like this, it also means that every time you make a decision of any kind, it will split again and again and again until eventually there will be hundreds of you living all these different realities. I believe you're understanding a lot of this, right? Absolutely, he's also understanding, but I know it's hard for our minds to accept it, so we don't dwell on this, that's why I called the books mind candy, you read them and you know, then you have to put the book aside and continue your life, otherwise, it could really confuse your mind. And I've also been told that if you don't put a lot of energy into that other decision, it will eventually dissolve anyway, so what you do now is what you've chosen, and it will be the life you focus on, don't worry about the other. I know that somewhere there's a woman, another person who never got into any of this, I don't know if she's sitting at home knitting and watching TV or what she's doing, but someone else of me has never been interested in any of this, I wish her good luck wherever she is."

How did your book "The Legend of Starcrash" come about?

"My book 'The Legends of Star Crash' was entirely based on sessions with a young woman. She was a college student and was majoring in music. She was really an organist, but more in the sense of a concert organist. She loved classical music, and that's what she was focusing on. But when we did the sessions, she would go back in time, way back in time. The legend of Star Crash tells the story of a spaceship from another planet. There were five of them, and they had been exiled from the other planet. They had to travel through space and establish a colony on another planet. As they passed through our solar system, one of these spaceships began to have problems and wouldn't be able to continue the journey. At first, I thought they wanted to land on the Moon to make repairs, but fortunately, they didn't. They had never seen a satellite like the Moon, so large orbiting a planet, so they thought it was a small planet. Instead, they crashed in the region between Canada and Alaska.

The other members of the crew realized they couldn't help them, so they continued their journey alone. But the people who crashed had to learn to survive. It's an incredible story because they had spent years and years on board the ship; it was like a generational ship, they were born and raised on that ship and were not used to the atmosphere, the sun. The sun's radiation was very hard for them to endure. Different leaders had developed in the group, and they had to live inside the remains of the spaceship to protect themselves from the strong sun. When they started reproducing, babies were born deformed or dead because they couldn't withstand the radiation. At that point, they had to make a decision: to survive, they would have to mate with the native populations of the area. When they did this, they really started the first Indian tribes in the American continent. When I went to Alaska and told them this story, the Eskimos told me that this is part of our legends about the history of our beginnings because the whole story has been passed down over the years. Years later, when they had a village with people living there, the man who was the hunter would tell the legends that were told around the fire in the evening, about how they had come there, where they came from, and how they found themselves in that area. They thought they were the only inhabitants of the world and had never seen other people. This turned out to be true when the Eskimos arrived and found that there were other people in the world. But this is the story of the beginnings of the Indian tribes and how they spread throughout the territory of the United States. It all began with a spaceship crashing thousands of years ago in that area, and this story is still present in the legends of the Eskimos."

What can you say about crop circles?

"I've been involved in crop circle investigations since 1992 when I first went there. I was inside my first crop circle with Alex Bartholomew, my English publisher. I had known about crop circles before that thanks to UFO conferences I was helping to organize here in the United States, but I don't want to go into the historical details because many of you probably already know them. It was in the early '90s, the late '80s and early '90s when crop circle designs began to become more complex. Before that, they were just simple circles, then, a few years later, circles inside circles, and then designs began to appear in the late '80s. When I went to England in 1992, I had already investigated crop circles for many years and knew all the investigators in the field. It's a fascinating field. In particular, Lucy Pringle is the one who flies over the crop circles and takes photographs. She has extensive experience in crop circle investigation. But I believe you mainly want to hear me talk about the circles, how they form, and what they are supposed to represent. There have been many stories about people making these circles, but the ones I've seen couldn't have been made by humans; they're too complex, and it would take hours and hours just to attempt to make them. The ones I've seen form in a matter of minutes. Lucy Pringle has also said that when she flew over a certain field, there was nothing, and five minutes later, when she returned, there was a complete design in the wheat or whatever cereal crop was present. What I've found in my work is that the real ones are not made by humans. I've been in some circles that were fake, and you could really tell the difference. Anything made by humans is approximate, while the real ones are perfect, very precise, and geometrically exact. The real ones, in my opinion, are made with energy. That's why no one has ever really seen anyone creating a real crop circle because there are no humans involved; it's done with energy. They even installed motion detectors and infrared lights around a field all night, hoping to catch anyone in that field trying to create a crop circle. But the next morning, they hadn't captured anything. They said that during the night, as the fog settled on the field, in the morning, there was a crop circle, and the motion detectors and infrared lights had not recorded anything. What I've found is that crop circles are made with energy. Some of them are beautiful complex designs, and over the years, I've seen more and more becoming increasingly complex. What I've found is that crop circles are a language. Our subconscious recognizes symbols, which are very, very ancient, dating back before humanity even had a language, before it had words, there were symbols. These symbols are so ancient that the subconscious recognizes them and knows what they mean. Most of the crop circles you will see will contain a message embedded in them. It's a language, and it's a language that your mind understands because concepts and symbols can contain blocks of information, whereas we have to communicate one word at a time, one sentence at a time, which is not how ETs and other beings out there communicate because they don't all communicate in that way. They communicate in concepts, so an entire concept can be in one symbol. When your mind sees it, it's seeing an entire massive block of information. This is how they communicate with us by putting blocks of information into one symbol. And this is transmitted to our subconscious at the cellular level when we see the symbol. You don't have to be in the crop circle to get this information, although it's really beautiful energy to be inside the crop circle, it's very peaceful and very beautiful. But you don't have to be inside the crop circle to get the information; you just have to see the symbol. These symbols have been photographed and disseminated worldwide for over 20 years. So, anyone who sees these symbols receives the information transmitted at the cellular level of the mind. I receive emails and letters from people all over the world who, for the past 20 years, have felt an uncontrollable compulsion to sit down and draw strange symbols, and they don't know where this compulsion comes from, they spend hours just drawing symbols. Other people say they lie on the couch at night in front of a window, and a beam of light comes in through the window directly to their head, and in that beam of light, they see all these geometric symbols. So, they want to know what's happening. The same goes for geometry and numbers; they are also a language. All this data is transferred to the subconscious at the cellular level to be there when we need it during this period of transition that we are going through. And when we need it, it will be there, and we won't even know where it comes from because it has been implanted in the subconscious mind at the cellular level."

Can you tell us more about UFOs and ETs?

"The topic of UFOs and ETs is very complex, intricate, and highly integrated. I'm not sure if I can summarize it in a few words, but I've been investigating ETs and UFOs for over 25 years and have written four books on the subject. So, I always recommend anyone interested in the history of ETs to read my book 'The Keepers,' which represents my 25 years of work with them and all the different phases we've gone through in trying to understand this fascinating phenomenon. In that book, I found answers to all the questions anyone might ever want to ask about UFOs and ETs. Later, I wrote 'The Keepers of the Garden,' 'The Legend of Star Crash,' 'Legacy from the Stars,' and finally 'The Primal Universe,' where we delved even deeper into the subject.

What I've discovered is that they are very positive beings, and there's nothing to fear. In 25 years, I've never had a negative experience with anyone I've worked with because I managed to understand why this is happening and the reasons behind it. Once you understand that, you see the bigger picture, and it's not negative at all because everything falls into place. So, I recommend anyone who wants to know more to read 'The Keepers' because in that book and 'The Keepers of the Garden,' we tell the story of how we were created by ETs at the beginning of the world, where we come from, our physical bodies, and how they were designed. They have been observing us and taking care of us since the beginning of our creation, and that's why they are often called 'The Keepers' because they have been watching our world and us for a long, long time and are very interested in what we do, just like you are with your children. In one of my books, they said they always wonder: 'Why do they always say we want to conquer the world? The world is ours, it always has been.' They said we can't do anything worse to ourselves than what we're doing. All they do is watch and shake their heads, trying to understand what we'll do next because when they created man, and I won't go into the details of this complex story, they thought, 'Let's give this beautiful planet a creature with intelligence and free will and see what it will do.' And of course, they always find themselves shaking their heads because they don't like what we've done. But we have free will; we have the freedom to make mistakes and do things we shouldn't, just as we do in our daily lives because this is the only planet in the universe that was created with free will. Many people have recalled past lives where they lived on planets where there was no free will, and they couldn't wait to get out of there and that life because it wasn't a very happy life. So, this planet is very unique in many ways, and one of the main ones is that we have free will.

Another of the directives they gave, called the 'primary directive,' when they created Earth, was the 'starship directive,' like in the Star Trek series. Star Trek was not fiction; the Star Trek directive of not interfering once you've created a civilization and it begins to develop, you can't interfere with the development of that civilization. So, they are bound by two laws: respecting our free will and not interfering with us. However, during the development of humanity, whenever Earth needed something, whenever it was evolving from primitive stages and beginning to have a civilization, they would come and live among the developing species. They would stay among us for many generations, for millennia. In every culture worldwide, there are legends of beings who bring culture, called 'culture bearers.' The culture bearer is the one who brings knowledge; for example, the Native Americans have their 'corn woman,' and every culture has someone who came to teach them how to do things. In all these legends, the culture bearer always comes from the sky or from across the sea, which aligns very well with ETs. They had to live among the people to teach them, and since ETs can live as long as they want, they have conquered disease, illness, and even death. They can live as long as they want and have remained among people for generations, generations, and generations. So, in all these cultures and their legends, these ETs lived among the people and taught them what they needed to do. So, from the beginning, they gave us what we needed at a given time. However, now that Earth is so overcrowded, when the next advancement, the next invention, the next idea is needed, they can't come and live among us anymore because there are too many people. So now the next idea has to be put in the atmosphere as an idea so that anyone who takes it and develops it gets the credit. Often we hear about many people worldwide working on the same inventions at the same time, and that's why all these ideas are put in the air, and anyone who takes them and develops them gets the credit. But it has to be in our timeline. That's how it works now, in our next evolution. We have to do it. Once they gave us a gift only once, and what we do with that gift is our free choice. Many times they gave us something we needed, and we used it in the wrong way. It was created for good, but we turned it into something negative, often turning it into a weapon or something else. But they don't want that. It wasn't what we were given. So, one day I asked them: 'Couldn't you come back and tell them: 'You're not doing it the way we told you'?'. They replied that it would be interference. They gave us the gift once, and what we do with it is our free choice. If they came back to tell us that we're not doing it correctly, it would be interference. So, we have to do what we want with the gift because we have the gift of free will.

This brings us to the present day. In my new books, 'The Three Waves of Volunteers' and 'The New Earth,' we are discovering a completely new perspective on UFOs and ETs, a perspective that we were not allowed to see before. Much of it has to do with vibrations and frequency. The Earth is changing now; we are entering a new dimension, and the vibrations and frequencies of our bodies have to change as we move into the new dimension along with the Earth. The Earth is entering its next incarnation, and it doesn't care whether humanity follows or not. It would be just as happy if we didn't because look at how we have damaged this beautiful planet. But if we want to go, we have to change our vibration and frequency to match that of the Earth as we enter the new frequency and the new Earth, leaving the old Earth behind. It's too complicated to go into all the details, it's all explained in my book 'The Three Waves of Volunteers and The New Earth,' because they had to ask for volunteers to come and help the Earth because the Earth is in trouble right now, and the people on Earth can't help because they are trapped in the wheel of karma, repeating the same mistakes over and over, the same karma that has plagued them, making them come back again and again to repay that karma without learning anything. There is much more to this story about why they decided to ask for volunteers, but I'll tell you this: many of the volunteers coming now have actually been ETs in other lives and have never been in a human body before. Imagine what it's like for someone to enter this chaos we call Earth without ever having been in a human body before. They don't like being here. We receive email after email, we have hundreds of thousands of them, all saying the same thing, and when I give lectures, most of the audience says: 'Now I understand, I thought I was the only person in the world who feels this way, but now it makes sense.' They never wanted to be here; they don't like Earth, they wonder: 'Why is there always violence, why do you keep hurting people?'. They don't want to be here; they always say: 'I want to go home, I don't know where home is, I just know it's not here.' Some of them have written to me and said they remember being children, standing in the kitchen talking to their mother and saying: 'I want to go home,' and the mother would reply: 'But you are home,' and they would say: 'No, it's not like that.' They know they never wanted to be here; they don't like being here; they'd rather be somewhere else. But many of these individuals have tried to commit suicide, and I always hear the same story from my clients, the same story over and over again, that suicide is not the solution because you have to come back and do it all over again with the same people, you don't get rid of them, you do your job, and then you can go home, away from all this. What I want people to understand is that these are ETs living in human bodies; they can remember being ETs, but the ETs are just another body, a different body, they are not alien foreigners, it's just a different body, they are not far from us, we are one soul, and the soul goes from one body to another to learn different lessons, wearing what I call a 'costume' or a 'suit' to play this role in this life at this moment. So, you have an ET body; it was just a costume, a part you were playing at that moment. Most of the people listening here have been ETs; this is nothing new, and we may go to other planets after leaving this one; it's all about the lessons you're learning in the school called Earth. So, they came to Earth to help, but when people talk about abductions and experiments being done on them, if we really look at the situation this way, all that ETs are doing is taking care of their own kind, that's what you need to understand. They are monitoring their own kind; they have to monitor the physical body because the energy of ETs is so completely different from that of humans that it needs constant adjustment. The energy must be regulated to see if it's surviving, if it's doing well in the human body, and that's why we talk about abductions. When they are taken aboard the spacecraft, it's to regulate the energy, make sure the body is in good health and capable of handling this challenging task it has taken on. This is what I want people to start seeing, ETs from a completely different perspective, and in the book 'The Three Waves of

Volunteers,' it goes beyond what other investigators have discovered. I know there are UFOs out there; I've seen hundreds and hundreds of images of them, but that's kindergarten stuff. We know they exist; we know they are watching us, taking care of us. But the other side is what the average person doesn't understand; they are just here to take care of you so that you can survive in this alien world we live in now, so that you can live on Earth. They are just taking care of their own kind; there's nothing to fear."

DOLORES CANNON'S BOOKS: A SUMMARY

Five Lives Remembered (1980)

"Five Lives Remembered" by Dolores Cannon is a book that outlines the author's initial foray into the world of past life regression. The book documents the early period of Cannon's career when she worked alongside her husband, Johnny, who was a hypnotist at the time.

The book narrates how, during a hypnosis session conducted on a woman named Anita, she and her husband unexpectedly discovered the phenomenon of past life regression. Anita, under hypnosis, began to describe past life experiences with extraordinary details, speaking in the first person and describing environments and historical contexts different from her current life.

In "Five Lives Remembered," Cannon describes five distinct lives remembered by Anita during the hypnosis sessions. These lives include existences in different time periods and locations, with unique life challenges and lessons. The book explores how these past lives influenced Anita's present life, highlighting themes of karma, spiritual learning, and personal growth.

The book is significant not only for its content but also for the role it played in Dolores Cannon's career. It was through these early regression sessions that she developed a deep interest in reincarnation and past lives, which she would later delve into in her research and numerous subsequent books.

"Five Lives Remembered" stands out for its narrative approach, making it accessible and fascinating to those who may be new to the concepts of past life regression and reincarnation. The book offers a window into how past experiences can shape our present and provides a unique perspective on the nature of human consciousness and spiritual memory.

Conversation with Nostradamus (1989)

"Conversations with Nostradamus" is a series of three books written by Dolores Cannon, with the first publication dating back to 1989. This series represents a unique and intriguing aspect of her work, in which she explores the prophecies of the famous 16th-century seer, Nostradamus, through regression hypnosis sessions.

In these books, Dolores Cannon uses hypnosis to connect her clients with Nostradamus himself, enabling direct dialogue with the prophet. Subjects under hypnosis, as claimed by Cannon, were able to communicate with Nostradamus and receive interpretations and clarifications regarding his famous quatrains, often cryptic and subject to multiple interpretations.

The narrative in Cannon's books focuses on the interpretation of Nostradamus's prophecies, many of which have been linked to significant historical events such as wars, revolutions, and political changes. Furthermore, Cannon discusses Nostradamus's predictions regarding the future, including themes such as global changes, potential natural disasters, and technological developments.

What is important is how Cannon connects Nostradamus's prophecies with contemporary and future events, attempting to shed new light on these age-old mysteries. The books not only delve into the interpretation of the prophecies but also explore the life and times of Nostradamus, providing insight into his persona and the historical context in which he lived.

The "Conversations with Nostradamus" series was published in three volumes, with the first volume released in 1989. The books have attracted both interest and criticism, with some praising Cannon's innovative approach to interpreting prophecies, while others question the methodology and conclusions. Nevertheless, the series remains a fundamental aspect of Dolores Cannon's body of work, demonstrating her continued interest in exploring unexplained and mysterious phenomena through regression hypnosis.

Jesus and the Essenes (1992)

Dolores Cannon explores the lives of the Essenes, an ascetic Jewish group living in closed communities characterized by a strong sense of community and deep spiritual practices. They are described as custodians of ancient teachings and knowledge, playing a crucial role in the preparation and education of Jesus.

The book also provides intriguing details about the lesser-known period of Jesus's life, between the ages of 12 and 30. According to information obtained through hypnotic regression, Jesus traveled extensively, visiting places such as India and possibly Tibet and Egypt. During these travels, he studied with spiritual masters and acquired wisdom that he later integrated into his teachings and mission.

Cannon also touches on the connections between Jesus and John the Baptist. John, presented as an influential member of the Essenes, would have recognized and supported Jesus's mission, contributing to paving the way for his ministry.

Another significant aspect of the book is the portrayal of biblical and historical figures in a more human and accessible light. For example, the description of Jesus's interactions with his contemporaries, how he taught and related to others, offers a more intimate and personal view of these historical figures.

Additionally, "Jesus and the Essenes" highlights the complex nature of the historical period in which Jesus lived, with references to various religious and political groups of the time and the tension between Jewish traditions and Roman influence in the region.

Finally, the book delves into metaphysical issues such as reincarnation and trans-temporal connections, suggesting that past experiences can influence our current lives in unexpected ways. Dolores Cannon uses these ideas to explore spirituality from a broader perspective, going beyond the traditional boundaries of religion and history.

In summary, "Jesus and the Essenes" is a unique blend of history, spirituality, and metaphysics that challenges conventional narratives and invites readers to consider a broader perspective on the lives of significant historical figures such as Jesus and the Essenes.

They Walked with Jesus (1994)

"They Walked with Jesus" (1994) by Dolores Cannon is a book that continues the exploration of past lives, focusing particularly on historical figures who lived during the time of Jesus Christ. This book follows "Jesus and the Essenes" and further delves into revelations about the times in which Jesus lived, based on information obtained through past life regression sessions conducted by Dolores Cannon.

In "They Walked with Jesus," the author documents the stories of two subjects, Katie and John, who, under hypnosis, vividly recount their past life experiences during the time of Jesus's ministry. These accounts offer a unique and personal perspective on daily life, cultural customs, and historical events of that era.

The stories told in the book describe direct interactions with Jesus, providing details about his teachings, miracles, and the impact he had on the people around him. These accounts offer a more personal and intimate interpretation of the historical figure of Jesus, different from the traditional presentations found in religious scriptures.

Through these narratives, Cannon attempts to paint a more complete and human portrait of Jesus, showcasing his profound emotional and spiritual impact on those who knew him personally. The book not only focuses on the miraculous aspects of Jesus's life but also delves into his everyday interactions and personal relationships with his followers.

"They Walked with Jesus" is considered a significant work in Dolores Cannon's research into past life regression, offering a unique perspective on the figure of Jesus and his era. The book appeals to those interested in spirituality, biblical history, and those seeking a deeper understanding of Jesus's influence on human history.

Between Death and Life" (1993)

"Between Death and Life" (1993), written by Dolores Cannon, is a book that explores the mystery of life after death, based on the hypnosis regression sessions of numerous subjects. This text offers an intriguing and detailed view of what might happen to the soul after physical death.

The book begins with discussions of subjects who remember their past lives and the process of death and what follows. Cannon uses these stories to outline a path that the soul follows after leaving the body. This path includes various stages, such as passing through a "tunnel" of light, encountering loved ones or spiritual guides, and a phase of "life review."

The author also addresses topics such as judgment and karma, suggesting that souls undergo a kind of evaluation of their earthly actions, but in a context of self-judgment and learning, rather than external condemnation or punishment. According to the stories recounted, souls analyze the lessons learned and plan future challenges for their spiritual evolution.

The concept of reincarnation is a central theme in "Between Death and Life." Cannon explores the idea that souls choose to reincarnate for various reasons, including learning, karmic healing, and assisting others. A detailed view is given of how souls decide their next lives, choosing the circumstances and challenges they will encounter.

The book also touches on communication between the world of the living and the world of spirits, suggesting that there is a continuous connection between these two realities and that spiritual guides and departed loved ones can offer guidance and comfort.

"Between Death and Life" is a thought-provoking text that offers a comforting and deeply spiritual view of death. It is a book that can be particularly enlightening for those seeking a better understanding of the cycle of life and death and for those interested in stories of past lives and hypnosis regression as a tool for spiritual exploration.

The Legend of Starcrash (1994)

"The Legend of Starcrash" (1994) is a book by Dolores Cannon that blends historical research with hypnosis regression to tell the story of a lost civilization. Through hypnosis sessions, Cannon explores the past life memories of one of her subjects who claims to have been a member of an alien civilization that crashed on

Earth.

The book focuses on the story of a spacecraft from another star system that, after crashing on Earth in ancient times, gave rise to one of the North American indigenous cultures. The protagonist of the story, through her hypnosis sessions, vividly recounts life on the spaceship, the dramatic crash, and the subsequent struggle for survival in a hostile and unfamiliar environment.

The author uses these narratives to explore themes such as survival, cultural adaptation, and the conflict between advanced technology and primitive life. The story also provides alternative explanations for some legends and myths of Native American cultures, suggesting that they may have roots in extraterrestrial events.

The book also delves into the realm of interpersonal relationships and the spiritual growth of the spaceship's crew members. Their evolution from highly technological beings to a community more integrated with nature and the Earth's environment is described.

"The Legend of Starcrash" is a mix of science fiction and spirituality, delving into theories of extraterrestrial life and their possible impact on human history. This text is for those interested in regression hypnosis, ancient astronaut theories, and stories of past lives. Cannon uses the narrative to propose an alternative perspective on human history, challenging conventional historical narratives with a viewpoint that combines Earth's past and stories of extraterrestrial civilizations.

Keepers of the Garden (1993)

"Keepers of the Garden" (1993) is a book by Dolores Cannon that outlines a unique narrative regarding the origin and purpose of humanity on Earth. In this work, Cannon utilizes hypnosis regression techniques to explore the past life memories of one of her subjects, who reveals information about extraterrestrial civilizations and their role in the creation and guidance of human evolution.

The main subject of the book, during hypnosis sessions, provides details on how advanced beings from other planets played a crucial role in human genetics and Earth's history. These "garden keepers," as they are called in the book, are described as well-intentioned entities who have helped shape human civilization and continue to monitor its development.

Through the subject's account, Cannon touches on various themes, including genetic manipulation, extraterrestrial interventions on Earth in ancient eras, and the idea that the human race has a kind of "custodianship" or guidance from these more advanced entities. This concept suggests that humans are not merely the result of natural evolution but rather a process guided and influenced by external forces.

The book also delves into topics such as spirituality, the destiny of humanity, and possible future directions of human evolution. Dolores Cannon uses the narrative to explore the idea of a universal consciousness and humanity's role in the broader universe.

"Keepers of the Garden" is particularly intriguing for those fascinated by ancient astronaut theories, past life regression, and potential interactions between humans and extraterrestrial entities. Dolores' book offers an alternative perspective on the history and destiny of humanity, presenting a narrative that combines elements of mysticism, spirituality, and science fiction.

The Custodians (1998)

"The Custodians" (1998) by Dolores Cannon is a work that delves deep into the experiences of close encounters of the third kind and alien abductions, exploring them through the lens of hypnosis regression. Cannon, known for her unique research methodology involving past life regression and communication with non-physical entities, offers a distinctive and detailed perspective on these phenomena.

In the book, the author recounts a series of cases of

individuals who have experienced close encounters or even abductions by extraterrestrial entities. Through her hypnosis sessions, she allows her subjects to remember and describe these experiences in detail, often hidden in their subconscious memory. These narratives include not only the physical experiences of encounters but also the communications and teachings received from the alien entities.

One of the central aspects of the book is the idea that aliens, or "custodians" as Cannon calls them, have an interest and an active role in human evolution and the preservation of planet Earth. They are described not as hostile invaders but as guides or custodians who assist humanity in its evolutionary and spiritual path.

Dolores Cannon also explores the broader implications of these interactions, such as their impact on human understanding of life, the universe, and our place in it. Topics such as genetics, consciousness, parallel dimensions, and the existence of other forms of life in the universe are touched upon.

"The Custodians" is, therefore, a book that appeals to those interested in UFOs and alien encounters but also to those seeking a more spiritual and metaphysical perspective on these subjects. Cannon uses her cases to explore ideas that go far beyond the simple account of alien encounters, inviting readers to reflect on the nature of reality, the meaning of human existence, and our position in the universe.

The Convoluted Universe: Book One (2001)

The Convoluted Universe: Book Two" (2005)

The Convoluted Universe: Book Three" (2008)

The Convoluted Universe: Book Four" (2012)

"The Convoluted Universe" series by Dolores Cannon, consisting of four volumes published between 2001 and 2012, is an exploratory and profound collection that delves into some of the most intricate mysteries of existence and the universe. Through hypnotic regression sessions, she explores themes ranging from past lives to encounters with extraterrestrial entities, from the understanding of ancient civilizations to the discovery of parallel realities and hidden dimensions.

In **"Book One,"** Dolores introduces concepts such as past life regression, out-of-body experiences, and the exploration of lost civilizations like Atlantis. This volume lays the foundation for deeper investigations that follow in the subsequent works.

In **"Book Two,"** the author delves deeper into her research on alien civilizations and their impact on human history. She also examines the phenomenon of "old" and "new" souls on Earth, offering insights into their evolution and their role in the broader cosmic landscape.

In **"Book Three,"** Cannon delves into even more complex and metaphysical concepts. She explores ideas like creating alternative realities through the power of thought, the existence of parallel universes, and the nature of time and space. This volume also introduces the idea of an imminent change in the destiny of humanity and the planet.

Finally, in **"Book Four,"** Dolores gathers and synthesizes the themes explored in the previous volumes, further exploring the connection between ancient civilizations and esoteric knowledge, the role of extraterrestrial beings in human history, and the future prospects of humanity in a rapidly evolving universal context.

In all four books, Dolores Cannon uses her sessions of regression hypnosis to explore and collect stories and testimonies that challenge accepted conventions about reality, taking the reader on a journey through the mysterious and the unknown. "The Convoluted Universe" series offers a unique and thought-provoking perspective on topics related to spirituality, metaphysics, and the paranormal, inviting reflection on the vastness and complexity of the universe we live in.

"The Three Waves of Volunteers and the New Earth" (2011)

"The Three Waves of Volunteers and the New Earth" is a book by Dolores Cannon that explores a revolutionary concept regarding the transformation of planet Earth and human evolution. Through her numerous sessions of hypnotic regression, Cannon discovers the existence of three distinct "waves" of souls who have voluntarily come to Earth to assist the planet in its transition to a new reality of higher consciousness, known as the "New Earth."

1. **First Wave**: This wave includes individuals born in the 1940s and 1950s. They are often solitary souls who struggle with the prevailing violence and aggression on Earth. They feel like outsiders and have difficulty adapting to conventional social structures. Many of them do not want to have children, feeling as if they don't belong to this world.

2. **Second Wave**: People of this wave are born from the 1960s onwards. They are here to serve as "human batteries" of positive and peaceful energy, contributing to bringing balance to the planet simply through their presence. They do not need to take specific actions; their energy alone is enough to positively influence others.

3. **Third Wave**: This wave consists of children born from the year 2000 onwards, often referred to as "millennial children" or "crystal children." They are highly advanced souls with a specific purpose and innate spiritual understanding. They are here to complete the transition process and help the planet evolve.

Dolores Cannon argues that these voluntary souls have

come from other worlds and dimensions where they have already overcome the issues Earth is currently facing. They bring with them special knowledge and abilities to help Earth transcend its "dark age" of conflict and disharmony.

The book also explores the relationship between these waves of volunteers and significant global changes. It describes how our planet is going through a phase of purification and energetic realignment, leading to a reality characterized by peace, harmony, and higher consciousness.

In "The Three Waves of Volunteers and the New Earth," Dolores Cannon provides a message of hope and an invitation to action. She suggests that everyone has a role to play in this transition period and that, by working together, we can co-create a new era for Earth and its inhabitants.

"Soul Speak: The Language of Your Body" (2013)

"Soul Speak: The Language of Your Body" is a book written by Dolores Cannon, focused on understanding and interpreting the signals and messages that our body sends to our consciousness. In this work, Cannon explores the idea that our physical body is in constant communication with our soul and higher consciousness, conveying important messages through physical symptoms, illnesses, and other bodily conditions.

The book is based on the premise that every physical ailment or disorder has a spiritual or emotional root. Cannon illustrates how physical symptoms can be interpreted as metaphorical messages that reflect emotional or spiritual issues. The goal is to help readers better understand the "language of the soul" so they can address the deeper causes of their ailments, rather than focusing solely on surface-level symptoms.

The author also emphasizes the power of the mind in creating and influencing our physical reality, including the health of our body. She highlights the importance of positive thoughts and attitudes in maintaining or restoring health and well-being. The book provides practical tools and self-inquiry techniques to help readers decipher the hidden messages behind various symptoms and illnesses.

"Soul Speak" builds upon many of the concepts developed in Cannon's previous books, combining regression hypnosis, energy healing therapies, and holistic medicine ideas. It offers a unique perspective on the relationship between mind, body, and spirit, encouraging a more integrated and holistic approach to health and well-being.

Ultimately, the book serves as a guide to better understanding oneself and one's health, suggesting that carefully listening to and responding to the messages of one's body can be a fundamental step toward physical, emotional, and spiritual healing.

A TEACHING DRAWN FROM THE REAL WORDS OF DOLORES CANNON: THE PATH OF FORGIVENESS AND LIBERATION - OVERCOMING KARMA AND FEAR FOR SPIRITUAL ASCENSION

During my career as a therapist and hypnotist, I have developed a deep belief and an innovative method based on the power of the mind. I have observed that illnesses are often the result of a mental process, and if the mind can induce illness, it can also heal it. My experience has taught me that every person has the ability to heal themselves using the strength of their own thoughts.

In my practice, I have witnessed miraculous healings while treating a wide range of illnesses. These events have convinced me of the crucial importance of the mind in the realm of health and well-being. I often tell my clients, "If your mind is powerful enough to make you ill, then it is certainly powerful enough to heal you." This is the philosophy that guides my work.

I have dedicated decades to perfecting this technique and teaching it worldwide. My goal is to help people recognize that they are more than just physical bodies; they are powerful beings with extraordinary abilities. I firmly believe that once these abilities are understood and utilized, we can completely transform our life experience.

Throughout my years of practice, I have explored concepts such as reincarnation and metaphysics, which were once entirely unknown. This journey has led me to better understand the complexity of human existence. I have come to the conclusion that we are all connected to a divine source, and our true home is not a physical place but a state of being that transcends material reality.

My technique goes beyond physical healing; it also extends to personal and spiritual growth. I teach people to free themselves from emotional and mental baggage that hinders their true purpose. I believe that by discovering one's passion and following one's destiny, one can live a life free from illness and aging.

Over the years, I have helped thousands of people better understand their origin and purpose in life. My message is simple: you are not limited by your physical body. You have a powerful mind and a spiritual connection that allow you to live a full and healthy life. This is the reality I teach and share through my work.

In my experience as a therapist, I have guided many individuals on a spiritual journey that led them to rediscover their divine origins. This regression process took them back to the moment when they were in the presence of God before embarking on their human existence. Through these journeys, I have learned that the human being is only a part of the entire spiritual journey, often the most complex and challenging part.

The individuals I have guided describe God as an immense energy force and a brilliant light, similar to the sun but without the heat. This light, which some call the Great Central Sun, is characterized by total and enveloping love. In this state, souls desire nothing more than to remain in that condition of absolute peace and beauty. In these moments, I often hear my clients express a desire not to be awakened, so intense is their experience of connection with the divine.

I have understood that our perception of God is limited; we can grasp only a small part of it. God, or the Source, is like the glue that holds the entire universe together. If this force were to weaken for even a moment, everything would disintegrate. Creation is an act of collective consciousness, and we, as human beings, are a part of this immense project.

During my sessions, I have explored the idea of the Big Bang as a metaphor for this divine process of expansion and creation. Every spark of this enormous energy explosion became a part of the universe, some transforming into galaxies, others into universes, and many becoming individual souls.

I have always emphasized that we are not our bodies; we have them only to experience this life. Everything we perceive is an illusion, a stage where we are producers, directors, and actors in our stories. We have the power to change the script of our lives whenever we wish.

Finally, I have shared with my clients the vision of Earth as a school, one of many in the universe, where souls come to learn and grow. Every lesson, every experience, is part of a broader curriculum that the soul must complete. I have seen people repeat the same lessons, life after life, unable to fully understand them. This cycle continues until we learn what is necessary for spiritual evolution.

Overall, my work has revealed that we are all part of a divine plan, destined to explore, learn, and ultimately return our experiences to the Source. This process of learning and spiritual growth is fundamental to our journey through existence. In my exploration of the universe and human consciousness, I have come to understand that we are all part of a beautifully orchestrated cosmic system. The universe, a vast entity governing everything, operates with infinite patience, allowing each of us to overcome our lessons at our own pace. There are no time limits for learning, but it is important to be aware that being stuck on a lesson for eternity while others move forward is a choice that depends on our free will.

I have discovered that one of the most crucial lessons is that everything in the universe has consciousness. Everything around us, from tables to floors, is alive and vibrates at a different frequency. This reminds us of our extraordinary ability to create. I have met people who identify as old souls, and I have reflected on how this may mean that they take more time to learn the various lessons of the universe.

During my sessions, I have also explored the idea that Earth is a school, one of the most challenging in the universe, where beings come to learn through dense and complex experiences. It is a unique planet, the only one in the universe with free will. I have guided people to remember lives on other planets where free will does not exist, and I have noted how they desire to leave those places quickly.

In every culture around the world, there are legends of culture bringers, who come from the sky or across the water to teach essential skills such as farming and the use of fire. These teachings were given when Earth needed to advance, always following the principle of non-interference.

I have understood that dimensions around us are multiple, each with its own life and cities, invisible to us because they vibrate at different frequencies. These dimensions would be deeply affected if our world were to be destroyed. An historical example of this phenomenon is Atlantis, an advanced civilization that reached a critical point where external intervention became necessary.

With the detonation of the atomic bomb in 1945, the universe's attention focused on Earth, leading to an increase in UFO sightings. I have learned that, to influence changes from Earth itself, volunteers from other planets were required, beings who had never lived on Earth before. This is unique to our planet: we forget our plans and contracts when we come here, but now, with the change in vibrations and frequencies, we are starting to remember, to reconnect with our original purpose. This change is accelerating, and we are bringing back lost awareness, opening new possibilities for growth and evolution.

In my work, I have observed that we are approaching a crucial point in the evolution of human consciousness. The "veil" that separates our perception from the wider reality is thinning, allowing us to receive information and insights that were previously inaccessible. The vibrations and frequencies of Earth are changing rapidly, making this historical period extremely significant.

I have found that many of my clients, during their sessions, access information about extraterrestrial lives or alternative dimensions. This has led me to understand that Earth is also a living being and, like us, goes through various incarnations. Currently, Earth is evolving into a new incarnation, entering a new dimension. This process is independent of human will; Earth will proceed with or without us.

To accompany Earth in this new dimension, we must change our vibrations and frequencies to align with her. This process is often described as "Ascension" and involves the transition from the old Earth to the new.

However, to participate in this transition, we must face two important challenges: releasing karma and overcoming fear.

I have explained to my clients that to release karma, forgiveness is necessary. Many people find forgiveness difficult, especially when they have suffered severe abuse or injustice. However, forgiveness is essential to break free from the past and move forward. Resentment and bitterness keep us tied to karmic cycles that we must repeat until we resolve them.

The second challenge is overcoming fear. Fear is an illusion that holds us back and prevents us from evolving. I have taught my clients exercises to confront and release their fears, as these are significant barriers on the path to ascension.

To help people practice forgiveness, I have developed an exercise that they can do even if the person they have a conflict with is no longer physically present. This exercise involves visualizing that person and communicating with them on a deeper level, beyond the constraints of time and space. This allows them to release repressed emotions and take a significant step towards forgiveness and liberation from karma.

In summary, my mission is to help people understand and navigate this moment of transition, encouraging them to elevate themselves spiritually and align with the evolving frequencies of Earth. This process of transformation is crucial for our collective and individual future.

In my therapeutic approach, I have developed a specific exercise to help people release karma and fear, two significant obstacles on the path to personal evolution. The exercise begins with a moment of deep introspection, during which I invite my clients to close their eyes and visualize in their minds the person they have an unresolved conflict with.

I ask them to imagine this person in detail, recognizing all the emotions that emerge. Then, in their mental vision, I guide them to say to the person: "We really tried, but it didn't work. Now, let's tear up the contract." At this moment, I encourage them to visualize the act of tearing up an imaginary contract symbolizing the karmic bond that connects them and throwing it away.

The next step is forgiveness. I tell them to address these words to the person in their vision: "I forgive you. I let you go and set you free. Go your way with love, and I will go mine. We don't have to be connected in any way anymore." This act of forgiveness is crucial to free oneself from emotional and spiritual chains that hinder personal progress.

After completing this step, it is important for people to also forgive themselves. Often, we forget that self-forgiveness is just as crucial as forgiveness towards others. Therefore, the last step of the exercise is to declare: "I forgive myself for..." and complete the sentence with any actions or thoughts that need to be forgiven.

This exercise is not just a mental practice but a deep emotional process. When done with sincerity and commitment, it can have a transformative impact. Once you release someone through forgiveness, that person no longer has any power over you. This process helps you detach from old energies and move towards a path of growth and personal evolution.

Discover a World of Knowledge and Inspiration

Visit www.libriutili.it

Dear reader,

We hope you have found inspiration and usefulness within the pages of this book. If your thirst for knowledge and personal growth is not yet satisfied, we have a special surprise for you!

We invite you to explore the world of LuminaLibria at www.libriutili.it, where a universe of books awaits you. LuminaLibria is an oasis for every type of reader, offering a wide range of genres that will enrich your reading experience.

For Little Explorers: Browse our collection of Children's Books and Stories for Children, perfect for igniting the imagination and curiosity of the youngest readers.

For Art and Relaxation: Let yourself be captivated by our Coloring Books for Adults and Children, a creative way to relax and express yourself.

For Personal Growth: Explore our Self-Help, Personal Growth, and Biography Books to inspire and motivate you on your life journey.

For Curious Spirits: Deepen your spiritual journey with our Spiritual-themed Books.

This is only a small part of what LuminaLibria has to offer. We believe that every book is a window to new worlds, ideas, and possibilities. Whether you are seeking adventure, knowledge, or inspiration, you will find a book that speaks to your heart at www.libriutili.it. **And remember, on the website, you will find books in Italian, English, and Spanish.**

Scan the QR Code below to begin your journey into the world of LuminaLibria.

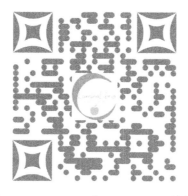

Thank you for accompanying us on this journey of discovery and growth. We are excited to see you explore even more with LuminaLibria.

Happy reading and continued exploration!

The LuminaLibria Team

Made in the USA
Las Vegas, NV
09 September 2024

95043254R00075